BORROWED NAMES

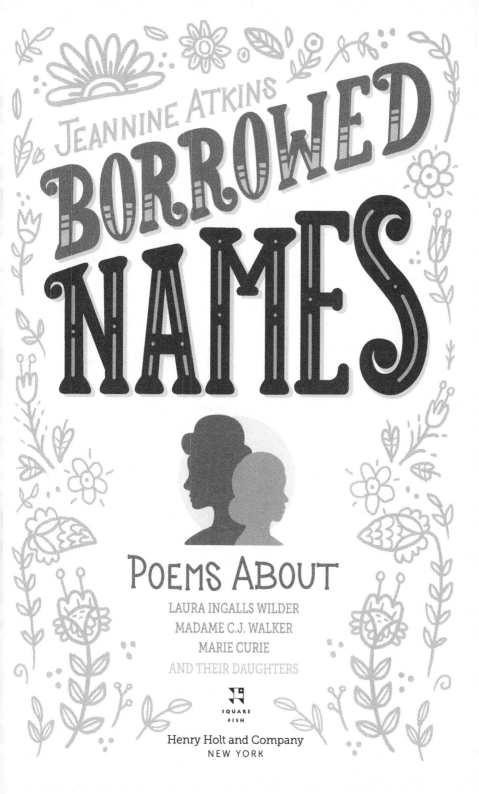

JEANNINE ATKINS

BORROWED NAMES

POEMS ABOUT

LAURA INGALLS WILDER
MADAME C.J. WALKER
MARIE CURIE
AND THEIR DAUGHTERS

SQUARE
FISH

Henry Holt and Company
NEW YORK

SQUARE
FISH

An imprint of Macmillan Publishing Group, LLC
175 Fifth Avenue, New York, NY 10010
fiercereads.com

Square Fish and the Square Fish logo are trademarks of Macmillan and
are used by Henry Holt and Company under license from Macmillan.

Our books may be purchased in bulk for promotional, educational, or business
use. Please contact your local bookseller or the Macmillan Corporate and
Premium Sales Department at (800) 221-7945 ext. 5442 or by e-mail
at MacmillanSpecialMarkets@macmillan.com.

Library of Congress Cataloging-in-Publication Data
Atkins, Jeannine.
Borrowed names : poems about Laura Ingalls Wilder, Madam C. J. Walker,
Marie Curie, and their daughters / Jeannine Atkins.
p.   cm.
ISBN 978-1-250-18340-8 (paperback)   ISBN 978-1-42995-940-7 (ebook)
1. Wilder, Laura Ingalls, 1867–1957—Juvenile poetry.
2. Walker, C. J., Madam, 1867–1919—Juvenile poetry.
3. Curie, Marie, 1867–1934—Juvenile poetry.
4. Mothers and daughters—Juvenile poetry.
5. Young adult poetry, American.   I. Title.
PS3601.T4885B67 2010   811'.6—dc22   2009023446

Originally published in the United States by Henry Holt and Company
First Square Fish edition, 2018
Book designed by Meredith Pratt
Square Fish logo designed by Filomena Tuosto

1   3   5   7   9   10   8   6   4   2

AR: 5.5 / LEXILE: 910L

To my daughter,
Emily Laird

CONTENTS

INTRODUCTION

ℐℬ THREE EXTRAORDINARY WOMEN were born two years after the Civil War ended, a time filled with grief, hope, and creativity. In 1867, African Americans could vote in the Southern states for the first time. Petitions for suffrage and other rights for women were signed and fought. Novelists and poets wrote about heroism in lives that had previously been overlooked. Painters depicted common scenes, too, often using looser lines and brighter colors than artists had before them. Inventors made the world seem smaller with swifter forms of communication and transportation. The transcontinental railroad was being built across a nation that grew still bigger when Alaska was purchased in 1867. That was the year that Laura Ingalls Wilder, Madam C. J. Walker, and Marie Curie were born.

Laura Ingalls Wilder would write books based on her childhood spent in log cabins, covered wagons, and on farms. A girl who planted and plowed cotton fields in Mississippi grew up to create a new name for herself— Madam C. J. Walker—and a wildly successful hair product business to go with it. Marie Curie left Poland to study chemistry and physics in Paris, and became the first person to earn two Nobel Prizes.

These three women not only shared a birth year but also a devotion to work and motherhood. They raised daughters who lived in a world that changed as quickly as theirs had, and who changed with it. The only child of Laura Ingalls Wilder inherited the family wanderlust and became a world-traveling journalist. Madam C. J. Walker's daughter helped manage her mother's business and supported the artists of the Harlem Renaissance. Marie Curie's older daughter carried on her mother's investigations of radioactivity.

For this book, I first read about the names, lessons, and homes the mothers provided for their children. Some gifts were gladly accepted, while others were reshaped or given back as daughters found their own ways to face celebrity, heartbreak, and love. I borrowed names and old stories, taking a bit here, putting another impression aside, turning history into poems. What did each daughter see in her mother's hands? I wondered: one pair worn by swinging hoes and holding back horses, another by scrubbing laundry and hair, and another by running scientific experiments. Details gathered meaning as I lingered over them, and I came to love what was small and tangible as much as the grand or public moments. I tried to be faithful to the known events and their chronology, but let my imagination fill in gaps the way we do when we look for truths hidden behind a face.

LAURA INGALLS WILDER

ROSE WILDER LANE

LAURA INGALLS WILDER
AND
ROSE WILDER LANE

CLEARING LAND

 LAURA INGALLS was born in the big woods of Wisconsin, but within a few years called many other places home: the Kansas prairies, a dugout by Plum Creek in Minnesota, covered wagons rolling westward, and at last a little house near Silver Lake in the Dakota Territory. There her family survived many blizzards, but one long winter they almost starved before Almanzo Wilder drove horses through the deep snow to get wheat and saved them all.

Almanzo began courting Laura when she was fifteen years old. Her father didn't object, though her mother believed Laura was more smitten with Almanzo's half-wild horses. At eighteen, Laura stood before a preacher, who agreed that a bride should promise to honor and love but not obey, and changed her name to Laura Ingalls Wilder.

Almanzo called his wife Bessie to distinguish her from his sister, who was also named Laura. Their daughter, Rose, who was born about a year after the wedding, would call her Mama Bess.

FIRE

Rose sees blood on the linen
before her grandmother plunges
the sheets in a tub. Pa scrubs dirt
from his hands. Whatever happens,
fields must be tended.
Mama Bess goes back to bed. Again.

Won't you get up?

Soon, Mama says, but Rose is hungry.
She puts a stick in the woodstove.
When the kindling, burning at one end,
turns too hot to hold,
she drops it.
Fire creeps
across the floor and laps the wall.
Air, once quiet and invisible,
spits sparks and orange flames.
Burning tablecloths twist like memory.

Where are you?

Smoke stings her eyes. Someone grabs her arm
and a fistful of forks. They rush
from the crackling, tumbling house.

Outside, Rose breathes the stink of burning chairs,
bedding, sacks of flour, jars of plum preserves,
beans left soaking in a yellow bowl.
The house becomes an oven, ruining
broom and dustpan,
the sewing box with its tomato-shaped pincushion,
an embroidered needle case, pewter buttons,
scavenged ribbon,
spools of crimson and sky-blue thread.

Little is saved but old dresses, silverware,
and a platter decorated with a sheaf of wheat, bordered
with a prayer: *Give us this day our daily bread.*

Under a blackened cottonwood tree,
its slim shade useless now,
Pa leans on his cane. *What happened?*

Mama says, *I shut the door to sweep,*
so dust wouldn't get in the kitchen.
A spark from the woodstove caught the floor.

Rose, three years old, cries, *I'm sorry.*

We built one house. We can build another,
Pa says. *What matters is we're safe and all together.*

Mama nods. *It was an accident.*

She turns to sort through what might be saved.
A wilderness of cracked china, ashes,
days when safety
was as common as a roof. She folds her black
wedding dress and tells Rose, *You did nothing wrong.*

But then she whispers,
We won't speak of this fire again.

The Second Secret

Rose's grandparents welcome the family
to their home where everything is kept in place
so Aunt Mary, whose blue eyes
can't see past their own shine,
knows which tin holds sugar and which flour
and exactly how many steps
to take between the ivy and geraniums she waters.
Rose minds her grandmother, who says,
Keep away from the woodstove.
Rose can feel even Aunt Mary's blind eyes on her.

Grandpa plays traveling songs on his fiddle
while Mama flips through brochures about farmland.
She, Pa, and Rose move to Minnesota,
where the cold winters deepen the pain in Pa's legs.
They journey to Florida to grow oranges,
but Mama finds Southern air too steamy.
Back in South Dakota, wolves howl. Rain beats
down the wheat and corn fields one summer.
The next July, flax and oats wither without rain.
Rose says, *I want a brother or sister.*

Hush. Mama Bess distracts her with a story
of a land where bright red apples grow.

She works for a dressmaker sewing buttonholes,
tucking in the short edges of cloth,
striving for stitches too small to see, trimming thread.
Her stiff hands move up and down
twelve hours till sundown,
six days a week. She earns a dollar a day.

At last she unclasps the needle, stops at the bank
for a one-hundred-dollar bill she hides
in the lap-sized desk Pa made and sanded smooth.
She says, *Don't touch.*

I know, Rose replies, obedient at eight, though
she loves to watch her mother's hand slide
over the slanting surface covered with green felt,
the crack of brass hinges when the lid is lifted.

Mama warns, *Don't tell a soul what's in that box.*

PRAIRIE

Pa cuts black oilcloth to cover and make curtains
for a carriage they load with a bedspring,
feather mattress, quilts, pots, Mama's desk,
and a coop of noisy chickens.
Is this their last summer on the prairie,
their last good-bye?
Rose throws her arms around Grandpa,
who smells of wood smoke and hay.
Grandma's apron smells of cinnamon and flour.
Rose touches Aunt Mary's hair, the color of flames.

Pa hitches up horses that pull them to the plains,
where the world is all land and sky,
the only sounds, birds, wind, grasses.
As dust billows, Rose bumps her mother's steady arm.
Pa lets Rose hold the reins.
She snaps them, willing the tired horses to trot faster.
Pa takes back the lead and shouts, *Whoa!*

They rest the horses at creeks.
Pa spits watermelon seeds.
Rose tries to spit farther. She and Mama Bess
hold up their skirts to wade.
Women come here for water,

but linger for words.
Where are you from? Where are you going?
Mama sniffs the heads of bundled babies.
She watches children
play shadow tag. The running water
seems to sing *not here, not yet.*

Some nights, Mama hauls out her lap-sized desk.
Rose watches her pearl-handled pen glide
like a lullaby. *What are you doing?*

I want to remember. Her hand makes small circles
before she shuts the lid on secrets.

As darkness and stars fill the sky, Mama talks
of olden days, back when she was called Laura
and won a prize for memorizing the most Bible verses.
One hard winter when her family ran out of coal,
they twisted hay to burn. After the flour was gone,
they ground wheat in a coffee mill to make bread,
almost as sweet as milk and honey.
When water got scarce,
they prayed for rain. They relied on self and neighbor.

Sometimes tales end with Pa
taking Grandpa's line: *Go west.*
Mama mimics Grandma: *Whatever you say, Charles.*

They laugh at words Mama never uses
except in these stories
where she's a child until she meets Pa,
who risks his life in a storm to get everyone food.
They find a preacher who agrees
to take *obey* out of the wedding vows.

One night Mama and Pa walk in the moonlight.
Rose is alone in the covered carriage, though neighbors
are a quick call away.
Rose runs her hands over the green felt,
then opens her mother's desk. The brass hinges squeak.
She doesn't find a corner of sky, but hears
the river roll like Mama's hand over paper,
a quiet claim: Here I am.

HIDDEN

The horse-pulled carriage rumbles through Nebraska,
the Kansas plains, and into Missouri's
Ozark Mountains
where Mama Bess says, *Stop.*

Rose stares at the woods and a log cabin
with no windows,
its walls plastered with old newspapers.
Mama smiles as if she can already see
crops turning green where trees stand,
a cozy house made from logs split to lumber.

Pa says, *Forty acres is a lot of work for one person.*

But not too much for two. Let's put down our money.
Mama pins a robin's-egg-blue ribbon
to her best black dress and talks swiftly:
A brook that runs all year long!
Four hundred apple trees already growing!

Possibility is as delicious as what's here
until she opens the writing desk
where she'd tucked the one-hundred-dollar bill.
Her face turns pale,
as if all four hundred trees topple.

The creek stops flowing,
the door of the log house is nailed shut.

Rose, did you tell someone we hid money?

No! You told me to keep it secret.

Did anyone come near when we were gone?

No, Mama.

*What about you, then? Did you take the money
for a game?*

I know not to play with money!

Of course. Mama slams the lid shut, risking a crack.
She tears off her good dress,
the one she wore at her wedding,
changes into her plain clothes, and sweeps.
We'll stay here. I'll look for work with a seamstress.
Someone always needs buttons.

A few days later, she opens the desk and looks again.
The bill is stuck in a crack where it must have slipped
during the rough journey. Relief is as quick
as the earlier fury. Mama puts on her black dress
but this time doesn't pin on the blue ribbon.
She runs as if everything might be lost again.

ROCKY RIDGE FARM

Mama pulls one end of the crosscut saw,
Pa pushes the other,
clearing the green hills for new orchards.
The scents of broken pine, oak, and balsam split the air.
They dig up rocks
and pile them for a fireplace.
Pa puts down the shovel
to show Rose how to crease a stalk
of grass and whistle. Mama sews Rose a dress
for the first day of school. Rose is proud
until girls stare as if it has too many buttons
or not enough.
Maybe the collar is the wrong shape.
Stuck-up Mary Ellen Tucker,
with gold glints in her hair,
chants, *Farm girl.*
Rose hides at lunch,
so town girls can't see she doesn't have
butter on her bread.
She pretends not to mind wearing her hair unbound
by the penny-a-yard ribbon
sold in Mary Ellen's father's store.
Rose claims, *I like going barefoot.*

She's glad to go home,
where Mama and Pa trade firewood for groceries,
plant strawberries and oats, peach and cherry trees.
They buy red chickens, a gray mule, and a cow.
Rose collects eggs from the henhouse,
breathing the sweet smell of damp straw.
Over time, forest becomes a farm. Mama changes
flour and water into bread, cloth into dresses,
and, at night, with spoken words,
her childhood into legend.

GENERAL STORE

Rose picks pails of blackberries and huckleberries
that she and Mama carry into town to sell,
walking past the cider mill
and canning factory to the hotel,
where men whittle and spit tobacco. Boys pitch
horseshoes on the common,
fish from the narrow bridge.

Mama trades the berries at the general store
where rakes, pitchforks, bolts of calico, candy,
molasses, and rifles are sold.
Rose smells puckered-skin apples
and barrels of pickles floating in brine.
Mary Ellen Tucker's mother stands
behind the counter chatting with Mrs. Reynolds,
whose little girls wiggle behind her back,
shift their weight in shoes
that are probably too tight.
Mary Ellen is home watching her sisters and brothers.
I don't know what I'd do without her. Mrs. Tucker
leans toward Mrs. Reynolds and whispers
about a lady who stole a peach pie,
then claimed it as her own

for the baked goods table at the church bazaar.
She gossips about pool halls
and saloons in Kansas City,
the dirt, the crime,
a girl sent away to an aunt's for nine months.
At the end of a sentence, she squeezes her lips
like a knot with no spare room.
Cutting cloth for Mama,
she smiles but takes note of how Mama's hands
are hardened by hoes. Rose knows she finds
the lilt of Mama's voice not familiar enough.
This town has too many rules and stories of fathers
and the fathers of fathers who grew up here.
As if staying in one place
is the sole measure of goodness,
as if ponds are better than running rivers or rain.
People in Mansfield want women to bear many children
to work fields or stock shelves.
An only child raises suspicion or pity.
When was fate a fair judge?

The little girls survey the glass-covered
case of red-and-white-striped peppermints
paper-wrapped taffy
licorice that turns teeth black

lemon drops.

Their mother says, *Choose one.*

Rose wants to fling open the glass door.
Hasn't anyone here ever said,
Take what you want. Take it all.

Rose follows the girls outside. Their braids
frame their heads as they lie on their backs
and stare at clouds. Mama Bess joins Rose.
I swear Mrs. Tucker joined the choir
just so she can face the congregation
and see who's skipping the sermon.

Rose is no longer a child. She rarely wears braids.
But she lies on the grass, too,
watches clouds until the three churches,
the newspaper office, the school,
the bakery, bank, and general store disappear.

LEMONADE AND GREEN PUMPKIN PIE

Grasses turn golden, are mown,
then gathered and bound,
stacked and stored.
By then more hay is ready to be cut.
Rose turns thirteen and wears dresses
that aren't waiting to be grown into.
She wins spelling bees,
milks the cow,
churns butter to spread on homemade bread,
pushes a plow, splits firewood.
At last Mary Ellen invites her to a party.
Rose sends her regrets. She won't say,
I'm going hunting for rabbits and plan to make stew.
But she finds her shotgun
and heads to the woods.
Wasn't this invitation
what she wanted? When did everything change?

The farmhouse is slowly built, room by room.
Pa frames windows with views of the brook.
Mama paints the porch where she tells stories.
She cuts an old striped shirt into quilt squares,
talking about the days
when Grandpa worked on the railroad.

We left loved ones, but we had each other.
She jams the porch with stories of ancestors
bearing guns for good causes. Even the dogs
back then growled only to warn, never on a whim.
Did I tell how you how your father made a way
through snowdrifts, some forty feet deep, to fetch food?

You told me. Rose asks Pa, *Is all that true?*

He winks at her above the shoe he patches.
He tells Mama, *You should put those tales*
down on paper.

No one would care. She turns to Rose.
Though one day you'll have children
who will want to know where they came from.

Does Mama think she can tell the future, too?
Rose's face burns.
She used to like the way these stories
of good people doing brave deeds
stitched her family together. Now she hears
only the refrain: *My life was rougher than yours.*
Rose never faced down a bear,
forded a flooding river,
ground wheat in a small mill for porridge,
or learned to be sweet to a blind sister.

When Mama says, *There's nothing like lemonade*
when you're thirsty, Rose leaps from the porch.
She's sick of lemonade and green pumpkin pie.
She runs through fields. A horse flips the mane
on her glossy black neck,
lifts her front legs high, gallops faster,
as if to say she'll stop if she chooses
but only then.
Rose loves the meadows and woods.
Trees, like imagination, leave spaces to slip through.

HOUSEKEEPING

The girl named for the rare rose on the prairie
who once *click-clack*ed in her mother's shoes
who tried on her aprons and dresses
stamps her feet on the mat
before she enters the kitchen.
Mama Bess sweeps with the diligence
of a criminal hiding tracks.
She presses red-checkered cloths to cover the table
so no one can see its beautiful wood.
She smooths an old quilt over the sofa so the fabric
won't fade, all the while humming songs
her father played on the fiddle, some of traveling
and some of home. She asks, *What did you do today?*

Rose's forehead turns hot. It's a trap, not a question.
Mama's goals are etched
on the skin between her eyes.
Mama's gingham blouse smells of ironing.
She crimps the edges of her pie evenly
dusts the china shepherdess
so its golden hair glows.
She can grow tomatoes without spots
and raise prizewinning chickens

but she can't add Rose to her collection of
strong father, patient mother, saintly aunts.
Rose can't pretend that silver linings can hold
back disasters. She won't be part
of her mother's perfect story.

MORSE CODE

Rose waits in the train depot that smells of metal
and oil. The dark room shakes as a train arrives,
grows smoky and loud with leaving.
The telegraph man clicks messages to places
she can't see. He confides, *I can get a job anywhere.*
As if that were worth all the afternoons bent over
a dark machine, his boots in one place.

Rose has learned all she can in the Mansfield school,
so she takes the train
to Aunt Eliza Jane's house in Louisiana
where she masters another curriculum.
She learns that a few
colleges are open to women,
but they're for wealthy East Coast girls,
not farmers' daughters from Missouri.
She returns home,
wanting another education
and different young men than she'll find
at chicken-pie suppers at the Methodist church,
ice cream socials, or piano recitals.
When Mama was her age,
she was courted by a hero

who saved not only her family
but the entire town
from starving one long hard winter.
Here, Rose suspects the lanky boys in overalls
would save themselves first.

MITTENS

Mama returns to the prairie
for her father's funeral,
then comes home with his old fiddle.
Rose inherits his wanderlust.

She studies Morse code,
stuffs her red flannel nightgown
in the bottom of a drawer,
and packs what she'll need in the city.

Standing by the porch, Pa leans
on his cane and scratches the black ears
of the goat who nibbles his trousers.

Mama asks, *Are you sure about leaving?*
Kansas City is so far away!

Rose says, *You traveled farther.*

Not alone.

I'm not taking horses and a covered wagon.
A young woman can be independent on a train.

Mama looks past the barn. *I always thought*
that would make a good spot for another house.
Maybe once you're married and have children.

Rose is astonished.
Lately she and Mama can hardly share a room
without finding fault with the other's hair
or hemlines. How could they be neighbors?
She says, *Farming isn't the only life.*

Pa coughs. *We'd better get you to the train.*

Mama scoops up her favorite small brown hen,
then puts her down. *Be good, but*
if someone acts peculiar,
don't waste time being polite.
Watch your pocketbook.
Be sure to get to bed at a decent hour.

Mama, you survived blizzards and droughts and disease.
I guess I can manage in a city.

Won't you be lonesome?

The last word falls back around the woman framed
by the doorway. Mama says, *Don't leave*
knives with wooden handles soaking in the sink.
Wipe your pens before putting them away.

Pa says, *Don't forget to write.*

Rose nods. She throws her arms around
her mother.

Love's language is imprecise,
fits more like mittens than gloves.

Mama turns as she has from so many little houses:
log cabins, dugouts, hotel rooms;
once her home was just a bed
with a makeshift curtain pulled around it.

PICNIC

As the locomotive speeds past sunflower fields
and redbirds, Rose won't look back. She finds
a future through the revolving glass doors
of the Midland Hotel. Working all night,
she taps her feet on the marble floor,
stamps out dashes, dots,
sends messages across the country.
Fingers flying, she telegraphs
thirty messages an hour
and earns $2.50 a week.
She needs more in Kansas City,
where a good hat costs four dollars.
For supper, she nibbles five cents' worth of peanuts,
sucking off the salt to make them last,
then takes on the day shift, too.

Charming, lonely salesmen ask her out for dinner
or dancing. She says *yes.*
Mama writes, *When are you coming home?*
Not yet, Rose answers at eighteen, nineteen,
then twenty.
She can't go back with nothing to show
but a few almost-out-of-fashion hats.

She meets a brown-eyed man
with a glance quick as a match catching fire.
Over dinner, Gillette Lane talks about rivers
he's crossed and cities he's seen. Candlelight
falls on the bones under his cheeks,
which curve like question marks.

One Sunday he rents a horse and buggy.
They ride through a park, discover a brook,
spread a blanket in the shade.
They eat hard bread, soft cheese, and apples.
The small bones of Gillette's hands press his skin
like roads on a map.
When they kiss, she smells wild mint, moss,
and pine,
as old loneliness, grudges,
imperfect face and body splash
away like water over rocks.

The next day they embrace as if at a long-awaited
reunion. They devote weekends to each other,
talking about music, moving pictures, motorcars.
He brings a bouquet, says *roses for Rose.*
Lush loose petals fall. They walk to the edge
of the woods where he asks,
Have you seen an ocean?

This handsome man cares more for trains
and traveling than houses. Rose hooks an ankle
over that of the man who knows the song
she loved as a child: *Not here, not yet.*
Overhead, birds spread silvery-blue wings
unclasping forgotten blue.

WEST

Come back home. Mama Bess sends a letter to Rose.
I'll sew you a wedding dress. I'll bake you a cake.

I don't need new clothes, Rose writes back.
Or vanity cakes
or gingerbread with chocolate frosting.
She won't risk Mama telling her beau
about burnt blankets and broken china
on the prairie.
Rose tells Gillette,
Let's walk in the ocean before we get married.

In California, Rose rents a room
with a washstand, bowl, and pitcher.
When she can't find work sending telegrams,
she sells canned fruit,
then works in a hardware store, doling out nails,
sacks of fertilizer, and seed. Men seem surprised
to see a woman stack pitchforks,
so why not become the first around to sell land?

Gillette meets her in San Francisco, where they sell
cattle ranches and oil fields divided into parcels.
They work from an office where their pens scratch,

sounding like saws pushing and pulling together.
His polished shoes shine as they stride across fields.

This place a farm? A potential buyer shakes his head.
There's not even a creek.

You can pipe in water.
Remembering how her mother's stories
turned wilderness into lands of milk and honey,
Rose chooses words to conjure orange groves
or fields fragrant with grapes. *What better life
could there be than picking fruit from your own trees?
Riding a horse home, where a dog sleeps on the steps?*

It's a lot of work.

Difficult for one, but two can do it together.

GHOST WRITER

Chinatown, Telegraph Hill, Fisherman's Wharf,
the canneries by the blue bay become theirs.
Here sunsets are luxury,
instead of marking exhaustion from a day
that begins before the rooster crows.
Rose and Gillette exchange vows.
Becoming Mrs. Lane, Rose hems curtains,
scrubs wooden floors,
sets red geraniums like her mother's on sills.
She puts a braided mat by the door
but won't ask anyone to stamp dirt off dusty shoes.

Everything seems possible,
perhaps half a dozen children,
like the brood her mother wanted,
and they'll travel, too.
Rose catches the California dream of fame
and won't drop it even after
war is declared in Europe. Few people buy land
when they don't know where they'll be next year.

Rose says, *People have to change with the times.*
Now she sells words instead of earth,
writing advertisements,

reports on accidents or crimes,
interviews with farmers and politicians.
She's pleased to push past the language of farming,
which begins with seeds and ends on a table.

Gillette can't find anything he likes to sell
as he did hills and valleys.
His back hurts. He spends long mornings,
then afternoons
on the sofa.

When Rose comes home,
she hands him a newspaper
folded to her stories and advertisements for jobs.
She worries about him, but grins to see
Rose Wilder Lane printed above features,
then on book covers below "as told to,"
though she lost track of which words
were hers and which belonged to Henry Ford,
who made a fortune on automobiles,
or to silent film star Charlie Chaplin. She labors
over legends that aren't hers,
like a woman stitching buttonholes
for dresses she won't wear. Borrowing
her mother's craft, she tucks away tattered edges,
glosses over impatience and disaster,

twists hard work and despair
into gilded endings.

Slowly, she fills an old cigar box with coins
and a bonus after writing
about Art Smith, daredevil pilot.
Strapped to the wing of his plane, Rose looks down
at San Francisco Bay.
In minutes, she soars as many miles
as it took her grandfather to travel in a day.
Her spread arms claim earth, water, sky,
everything she sees.

PAPER AND BLOOD

Had the black-haired butcher flirted
or was he just kind?
Rose wonders as she enters the small apartment
with fifteen cents' worth of lamb chops.
Gillette is asleep on the sofa.
If he can't find work, can't he at least sweep the floor
and wash the dishes? His soft hair curls over his ears,
but he won't let her come near with scissors.

She picks up the mail from the floor,
sets aside bills, refuses to see how much money
they owe, not tonight.
She opens a letter about how her mother
cans, pickles, harvests wheat and oats,
milks the cows,
collects eggs from the brown leghorn chickens.
Mama joins the local Red Cross chapter
and sews undershirts for soldiers.
There's news about the county fair,
the horse races and pie-eating contests.
Your father won first place and fifty cents
for the best millet which, you know,
we use for chicken feed. I'm not boasting,
but we got two dollars for the best fat steer.

Rose folds the letter back on its old creases.
She curves a hand over her belly,
which is turning hard and round.
She's tired. She's hungry. *What's wrong with me?*
Why can't I be happy with what makes others happy?
She unties the strings wrapped around the meat,
unfolds bloodstained paper,
and cries for no reason.

BIRTHDAY

Coming home, sweet fragrance
greets her before she sees jars crowding the table
and windowsills. Pink, red, and yellow blossoms
are strewn on the sofa. *Roses for Rose,*
Gillette says. She kisses him, then opens the cigar box,
which smells of tobacco, balsa wood, and old silver,
empty now.

She doesn't ask, *How will we buy food for supper?*
She won't say, *We have a child coming to think about.*
Instead, she gathers the flowers in her arms, rushes
down to the street, offers single stems to passersby.
She colors the truth—what else can she do?—
chants, *A dime for a rose, please. For charity.*
Well, it was money for their supper,
maybe not such a lie.

BOX OF RASPBERRIES, UNEATEN

Come visit, Mama, Rose begs in letters.
Pa will love the sunshine.

How can we leave when there are chickens to feed,
cows that need milking,
strawberries or apples to be picked?

As if no one else can toss seed to the chickens.
As if anyone else would forget the cows
and leave strawberries to rot.

I'll come after the baby is born,
Mama pens in her neat round script.
Did I tell you, I've started a bit of writing, too?
She encloses clippings of columns about farm life:
tips on thrift and how to coax hens to lay more eggs,
advice about honesty and gratitude,
how to cope with gossip and rocky soil, how to grow
prizewinning corn, carrots, tomatoes, potatoes.
Advice, Rose thinks, on everything
but how to stand the boredom.
She kisses Gillette's neck. *Let's walk on the beach.*

It's too far away.
He rolls over, his face pressing the sofa's back.

Rose slams the door on her way out.
She walks up a steep winding street,
wonders if she's wrong to get so angry
about tidy shelves and clean floors
and how her husband never even gets to the barber.
She stops at the grocer's,
buys a carton of raspberries for their dessert,
a folded newspaper.

After she steps out the door, blood gushes
down her thighs, trickles over her knees.
Her heart beats hard
as if she were running.
She presses her thighs together,
hunkers over, makes it to a bathroom, where she sobs
until she's certain nothing is inside her.
Through a fog,
she finds her way to a doctor. His eyes tell her
she's lost not only this child but perhaps all others.
I'm sorry, he says. *It's no one's fault.*

INTERNATIONAL EXHIBITION, 1915

Too late, Mama Bess takes the train west, letting
Pa care for the dog, cows, chickens,
and vegetable garden.
She admires Rose's gold band. This is the first
time they've seen each other
since she became Mrs. Lane,
so how can Rose say that her marriage is troubled?
Tomorrow, she will show her mother the city,
but tonight she has a deadline,
so she hands over a book with
her name beneath the title.
Mama folds their laundry,
bustles around Gillette,
straightens doilies on armrests,
dusts the trunk they use as a table,
sweeps under his feet.
She crunches old newspapers
and scrubs the windows with vinegar and water.
For supper, Mama tastes
the Chinese food Rose brings
without wrinkling her nose,
but the next morning she complains,
Can't a good fresh egg be found in San Francisco?

The next day at the International Exhibition,
Mama lingers in the Missouri rooms.
Imagine, we're second only to California in prizes.
There are more authors from Missouri
than any other state!

They wander through a Navajo village
where mothers and daughters
weave rugs or shape pots. Rose turns her head
from babies in strollers.
She and Mama don't squat to smile at toddlers.
People whisper about an elegant dark-skinned
visitor, said to be the first woman
to earn a million dollars.
Henry Ford lectures about the Peace Ship
he sent to Europe.
Mama Bess says, *I don't suppose you'll introduce me.*

Mama, Mr. Ford and I aren't exactly friends.

But you wrote about him!

I researched. Do you like those Model Ts?
When I write my bestseller, I'll buy
one of those tractor things for Pa.
It would make plowing easier.

He'd be happier if you came home.

Not yet.

I wish things could be the way they used to be.

Nothing was the way you remember.

A foghorn wails.

ANOTHER DAY

Rose comes home from work
and finds Gillette
pouring tea for her mother.
He says, *You never told me*
what a storyteller she is. No wonder
you became a writer.

Mama says, *Rose doesn't care for my little tales.*

I always liked them. Gillette's right.
You should write them down.

Who would want to read about us?
Mama picks up
the book Rose wrote
about Henry Ford and his motorcar factories.
Folks want to read tales of men like him,
a farm boy who made a fortune.

There are other stories.
Mama, we could work together.
Write casually
as you write letters to me,
but skip the advice.

Writing books is a risky business.
You can't know when words will come
and when they won't.

But you've worked on farms
through droughts, locusts, and prairie fires.
You know how to take a chance.

PACIFIC

Two women lift their skirts over the blue ocean.
Rose picks up a stone, wave-smoothed,
aches with the possibility and waste in bending
for beauty. Waves crash. Her hands shake
as if holding a carton of raspberries
she'll never taste. Her knees wobble.
You wanted a house next door filled with children.
Mama, I'm sorry. I can't.

You have no cause to be sorry. Rose, I understand.

No one understands!

That's what I thought when I had a baby
who died at twelve days old.
Mama digs her toes into sand
that the fierce sea sucks back. Pebbles clatter.
My mother lost a son, too.
Three generations, we all lost baby boys.

I didn't know.

You were just three, too young to remember
that poor baby, sick right from the start.
We never even named him.
It was just before the house burned down.

Mama, what happened that day?
Rose can't forget blazes, blame,
the stench of burning chairs, china, and dresses.
Memory is an acrobat: With each spin and tumble
new pictures shift into view.
There's more she wants to say:
Am I a terrible wife? Can I do anything right?

That fire was nobody's fault. Mama wrings cold
salty water from her skirt.
She slips her shoes back on,
not bothering to shake out the sand.

ANOTHER OCEAN

Rose spills the old cigar box,
spends all her savings on a motorcar.
She and Gillette head east to look for new jobs.
They write and sell,
short stints in Ohio, Pennsylvania, Massachusetts.
They drive north to Maine and walk on coastal paths
by rocks and flimsy-petaled roses
that thrive in salt air. Waves crash below, a rhythm
Rose hears as *not here, not now, not yet.*

Gillette says, *Maybe it's time*
we settle down somewhere.

Settle: that was never a word Rose loved,
like the sounds of surf striking rocks.
Maybe a baby would have kept
them in one place. Maybe not.
Her husband's beautiful brown hair
is too long over his ears and thin on top. He grabs
a fistful of wild roses, breaks the thorny stems,
and holds them toward her.
Before he can say *roses for Rose*—she can't bear it—
she grabs the bouquet and lets flowers fall
by his dusty shoes.

She wishes the name she'd taken
had been only on loan.
With a pricker-scratched fingertip, she traces
the bones under his cheeks, curved like question marks.
She keeps her eyes
on the blue-gray sky merging with sea.
Even the ocean that goes on and on
can't console them as they say good-bye.

POSTCARDS

Rose sells the automobile, keeps the typewriter,
takes a train to New York City. She cuts her hair
in a fashionable bob and shortens her skirts.
She finds work,
attends concerts, visits museums and art galleries.
She falls in love with paintings brilliant
with shades of scarlet and crimson
she's never seen before, and soon
shares a Greenwich Village apartment
with the artist.
The two women can't afford to pay for heat.
Rose heaps blankets on her shoulders
and types news and a novel.

When the Great War ends,
the Red Cross hires Rose
to report on what people in Europe need now.
She lugs her typewriter through France, England,
Italy, and the Middle East,
where battles have stopped, but poverty remains.
Rose writes grim stories
so donors can give happy endings.
She mails postcards from Vienna and Prague.

In Poland, hungry children accept buckets of milk
and chocolate and kiss the Americans' feet.
Rose joins Red Cross workers
in the home of a countess who, since her maid left,
sleeps in her shoes:
she can't unfasten them herself.

A daughter's circle winds wider than her mother's.
Rose wonders if the old town
is as small as she remembers.
She misses the gray mule,
the dog jumping on her knees,
the cluck of chickens wobbling on thin legs,
but how can she go back
with no husband, child, or fortune?
She's written hundreds of articles, a few books,
but no words that echo her heartbeat or pulse.
Does her mother ever haul her writing desk
out from behind old egg boxes and jelly jars?
Does she remember
trees she'd chopped and sawed,
the green branches that bowed overhead,
does she hear the past hum with promise and joy?

Rose sends money home: *Mama, hire someone to help*
with farm work so you'll have time to write.

You're like your grandfather, Mama writes.
He always thought he'd find something better
somewhere else.

Rose wonders if he did.

ALONE

Constantinople. Baghdad. Berlin.
Where now, where next?
Paris. At a café on the Champs-Élysées,
Rose and her new friends
belt show tunes until midnight.
They stroll by the Seine,
admire the stained glass and gargoyles of Notre Dame.
Years move forward, fold back,
revealing the daughter she should have been
and wasn't, then was. She lives briefly in Canada,
the Caribbean, Egypt, and Iraq. She meets other men,
other women, says more good-byes.

In the mountains of Albania, she shivers in a tent,
longing for her old red flannel nightgown.
One morning she passes a peasant on a corner
surrounded by wilting flowers.
She thrusts a bouquet toward Rose,
who asks, *For charity?*

My children are hungry.

Rose gives her all her coins.

Have the friends
who sang in the French café gone home,
married, had babies,
do they sing lullabies instead of show tunes?
The children who hugged her knees, grateful
for milk and chocolate,
have grown up. The countess surely has learned
to unfasten her own shoes.
Rose has slept under stars
and in too many trains.

CIRCLING HOME

Distant hills are green and yellow.
The old hitching posts
are gone now that more motorcars than horses
travel Mansfield's roads.
Rose strides past cornfields and a pasture
where a black mare gallops. White blossoms scent
the air as a hard wind rips off petals,
flattens them to the ground.

The house and split-rail fences look smaller, but
trees have grown. Goats hobble over rocks
and bend their long necks to nibble grass.
Red-brown chickens flap their wings.
Rose kicks dirt from her shoes
without being reminded.
She pries open the warped door,
hugs her father and mother.
Mama gives her a warm supper
and tells how they plowed up the old crops
and planted meadows with grass and clover.
They sold the cows but keep a small herd of goats.
Rose offers to help with dishes,
but Mama shakes her head,

scrubs the skim of color left by jam in the sink.
Rose goes upstairs. A folded flannel
nightgown lies on her bed. She stuffs it in a drawer,
then goes back to the parlor where the snoring dog
curls on a braided rug.

Her mother sits by cotton curtains
that smell of bleach. She looks out the dark window.
Too much work always kept her from watching
petals fall off an apple tree,
or even admiring the shapes of carrots
cut for soup, the clean smell of celery.
Now for almost half a minute Mama
attends to gazing.
This is a woman Rose hardly knows,
the scent of jam on her pale hands.

TOWN GIRL

Mama points out that the roof leaks,
a pipe has rusted,
the scuffed floors need to be sanded
and waxed. Shelves are stocked
with pickles, grape jelly, and preserves,
but the china shepherdess has cracked.
The glue makes a narrow yellow line.
Rose vows to change their lives,
typing what she hopes
will be a masterpiece.
She feeds the chickens, checks bylines
before scrunching up newspapers,
pours vinegar into water, scrubs the windowpanes.
She uses dishwater that Mama
says is too cool,
and when she sweeps, ignores corners.

Rose goes to the general store
where a slim blond girl dips
her hand into a barrel of peppermint candy.
Didn't Mary Ellen Tucker get older like everyone else?
Rose looks again
at the woman in front of stacked ammunition,

tobacco, and orange notebooks, a nickel apiece.
This is Mary Ellen. She introduces Rose
to her daughter,
then leans across the counter, compares the crusts
of ladies' lemon pies,
whispers about a girl sent to Kansas City:
She says the baby she's expecting is the son of God.

Who knows? Rose says. *Maybe the baby is the Messiah.*

That girl knows nothing about angels.
Don't you read the Bible?

Why not believe your neighbor instead of a book?

SMOKE

Words are spare and functional as umbrellas,
but they are for more than shelter. Rose types
most of the day. When her novel sells briskly,
she buys a blue Buick she names Isabelle
and teaches her mother and father to drive.

Pa says, *I prefer horses.*
They listen when I shout whoa!
He doesn't want a tractor. Claims the house they
have is fine. But Rose hires a boy to clear the land
where her mother had set a different dream.
She hires carpenters to put up beams,
joists, and rafters to hold up walls and roofs.
She examines planks of wood for flaws
and studies blueprints, shingles, and tiles.
She decides to change the height of the ceiling,
the angles of faucets.
The plaster was tinted the wrong shade of white,
the lacquer on the floors is too shiny
and must be redone. She hires electricians,
then stores the old kerosene lamps in the barn.
She orders a writing desk so big the doorway
is cut to fit it through.
She buys a globe, a terrier puppy, a doormat,

and helps her parents move into the new house
next door.

Sitting by Mama Bess on a spotless sofa,
uncovered by a quilt,
Rose holds a match to a log
in the fieldstone fireplace.
Sparks sting her hands. The room brightens.
Mama, do you like this house?

Of course. Not that I ever complained
about the old one.

I wanted to pay you back
for the farmhouse I burned down.

What house?

Mama, you remember.
When I was hardly three on the prairie.
I dropped a stick by the woodstove.
Everything went up in flames.

You were a child! You didn't know better.
Anguish catches in Mama's throat.
I was sleeping after dawn,
leaving you all alone in the kitchen.
What kind of mother does that?

You'd just given birth. You buried a baby.
Of course you were worn out.

Tired, that's a poor excuse. Can you forgive me?

Rose reaches for her hand. *Nothing is unforgivable.*
At last she understands.
That fire was no one's fault.

TEACHING HER MOTHER HOW TO WRITE

Rose lifts the jar of daisies,
the salt and pepper shakers,
throws off the red-and-white-checked cloth.
The table is bare. The beautiful wood glows.
She sets her typewriter near a window.
Mama's broom swings
to the rhythm of its *ca-click-clatter.*
Rose gets up for a drink of water, a look at the sky.
When she comes back,
Mama trails her fingertips across
the keyboard's letters rimmed by silver circles.

Rose offers, *I'll teach you to type.*

I'm sixty. Too old to learn something new.

Then use a pencil and paper.
I'll type your stories when you're done.

Who would care? You've seen the world,
but what have I got to say?

You cut down a patch of woods,
chopped logs, sawed lumber,
and built walls.

Not everyone can turn a square of cloth into a dress.
You and Pa made something from almost nothing.

It doesn't mean I can put that on paper.

Pretend you're talking to me like when I was little.
Remember one thing—the price of wheat,
the scent of violets or vinegar pie—
and memories jammed behind may unroll
like thread off a spool.

Rose unties her mother's apron.
Whatever happens now
here's the grace:
A writer can change even a burning house,
depending on where she begins or ends her story.

Mama hauls out her old writing desk—
its wood worn, the green felt faded—
and sharpens a pencil.

Broken Reflections

They rest their feet on trees that changed
to wood planks, by fieldstones that became a fireplace.
After writing, they pause for lemonade
and sponge cake.
Rose reads, then asks, *Can you really remember*
exactly what happened when you were three?

I remember.

No one will believe you can recall every word spoken
sixty years ago. Let's make Laura two years older.
Then when she gets to meeting Pa, she'll have a beau
eight years older, instead of ten.

I've never lied.

Rose picks a crumb from the willowware plate,
with its pictures of blue birds and bridges.
She says, *Words are like mirrors:*
A reflection is never the real face.

Of course I'm not keen to say we drank from the creek
without first boiling the water.
Nothing was wrong with that water,
but I'd hate for folks to think we were careless.

Let's say the water came from a spring. And if you
can't remember whether you saw the panther in fall
or winter, make up a season.

As fire dances into ash, as life merges into memory,
the woman with a sun-wrinkled brow
becomes the girl who stuck out her chin
when faced with locusts,
drought, and girls who laughed at patches on her dress.
Rose knows she still loves blue.

NOT TODAY

Mama says, *There's too much housework.*

Please. Do not get sidetracked
by shirts that need pressing.
There will always be fine grime
on the china on the mantel,
corn to husk, cherries to pit, apples to core.
Ignore them. The dream begun under a tree
is sweeter than stories you tell yourself
over dirty dishes.
Life tempts most away from paper and pen,
but gently bring yourself back.
Who can resist gingerbread
with chocolate frosting,
but do you need to bake it now?
If you must get out pots and pans,
come back and invite your distractions—
cinnamon, ginger, and nutmeg—onto the page.

SHEARS

Stories unroll like a bolt of cloth over the table.
When the pattern looks smooth, Rose turns
the fabric inside out, opens her scissors.
She craves the first stroke of blades slicing
a clear way through cloth.
She is the invisible shaper
behind the page, choosing where to begin
and end this particular history.

It took weeks to write that chapter! Mama snatches
the orange notebook from Rose's hands.

Let just an edge peek out.
Rose takes back the notebook.
Begin with extravagance, but be ready to trim.
No one knows the name
of the editor, the ghostwriter,
but the woman no one sees can create, ruin,
or tailor scenes so everything ends happy at last.

They put in poverty, blizzards, prairie fires,
leave out the milliner who cried
as she tied ribbons around hatbands,
chose feathers, folded paper flowers, mourned

the husband who'd left her.
Was she worse off than wives
who rode in from their farms
to drag drunken husbands back from saloons?
That's not our concern.
Or the sisters who fought
over who should inherit the family farm?
Don't mention the children
who froze to death on Plum Creek,
the murderers in Kansas.
One family has troubles enough.

They won't write about the baby
who was buried.
Even good dogs must die,
but such a shame that Jack was bartered.
Let's let dear old Jack spend his last night at home
curled in a peaceful sleep.
Truth is as much justice as fact.
*We can't include everyone you met or
even those who shared your home.*
We'll show just one beau,
the one Laura will marry.
Cut the other young men
who ever asked her to dance.

Mama, what kept you moving forward
through droughts, wild animals, loneliness?

We had no choice. Sadness was as dangerous
as panthers and bears.
The wilderness needs your whole attention.

TRUTH

Sometimes they can hardly tell who wrote which word,
who shaped which sentence. It doesn't matter.
Words change as Rose taps the keyboard,
types chapters she wraps in brown paper.
She sends off *The Little House in the Big Woods*.

Months later, she holds a bound book,
breathes in paper like a bouquet, strokes the cover,
smooth as petals, around her mother's name:
Laura Ingalls Wilder.
It's all yours, Rose says, though every sentence
was touched by both mother and daughter.
Words blurred and brought them together:
wolves, bears, panthers,
rabbits, snakes, and gophers,
a girl who slapped her yellow-haired sister,
endured the nearly unbearable stillness of Sundays,
Christmases where cousins feasted
on maple syrup candy
and at night, lined up like pins under one quilt.

There are more stories before they reach
the young woman who refused
to say *obey* in her marriage vows,

the mother who shouted *Where are you? Run!*
and grabbed an armful of clothing, a fistful of forks.
The past is more than ashes and char.
Maybe one person can't shape truth
into a story,
but handing orange notebooks back and forth,
a mother and daughter put ordinary girls into history.

LEGACIES

🐦 BIOGRAPHERS AND LITERARY CRITICS have examined the manuscripts passed between mother and daughter and noted how, as Rose Wilder Lane typed her mother's handwritten stories, she added detail, dialogue, and description. She trimmed in a way that most agree enhanced the pace and rhythm. Many believe that the eight books about the little houses where Laura Ingalls Wilder lived would not have been as beloved without the changes made by her daughter.

When working on these books during the 1930s, Rose lived mainly in New York City, though she often visited her old home in the Ozark Mountains of Missouri. She later settled in Danbury, Connecticut.

After the deaths of her parents, she focused on writing articles and traveling. When she was seventy-eight years old, she rode a helicopter over South Vietnam, working as a foreign correspondent. She died in her sleep at age eighty-two, just days before a planned trip around the world.

MADAM C. J. WALKER

A'LELIA WALKER

MADAM C. J. WALKER
AND
A'LELIA WALKER

BENDING HER BACK

SARAH BREEDLOVE didn't like talking about her difficult past, so little is known about the years before she took the name of Madam C. J. Walker. She was born in Louisiana in 1867, two years after the end of the Civil War. Her parents were former slaves who still planted and picked cotton, having little opportunity to find other work. Both died by the time Sarah was six. Aunts and older sisters took turns watching over her, but they had little time or money, and Sarah, who'd begun working in the fields soon after she could walk, went to school for only a few months. To get away from the cotton plantation, she took in laundry: dipping, draining, twisting cloth into knots, wringing out hope.

Sarah married at fourteen. Three years later, she held her newborn whom she named Lelia, but who would later choose to call herself A'Lelia. After the girl's father died when she was about three, Sarah promised her only child, *Everything will be different for you.*

Saturday in Missouri, 1896

A'Lelia and her mother cross brick streets
and train tracks. The basket of folded clothes
between them smells of soap and starch.
Opening a back door, A'Lelia glimpses
a shining stove. Glasses sparkle on shelves.
Down a hall, a black dog sleeps
by a man unfolding a newspaper.
Whose father is he? A'Lelia asks. *Is he kind?*

Momma shrugs as she goes down the steps, knocks
at another door no one answers. The clothes
are clean. That's all customers want.

A'Lelia and her mother carry the empty basket
toward leaning porches, saloons, dance halls,
a fortune-teller with bent cards and chipped teacups.
The yellow awnings on a barber shop catch dust.
The sun sets over steamboats on the muddy river
that A'Lelia can smell, though it's too far to hear.

Inside their home, clotheslines crisscross the room.
The washtubs are drained but
the room stays steamy
with white folks' sheets and shirts.

When A'Lelia says, *I'm hungry,*
Momma fixes supper.
She puts the last good potato on A'Lelia's plate,
turns over the potato she serves herself
to hide its bruise.

Once three plates were set on this table,
but Momma always filled A'Lelia's first
and kept watch on portions. Her girl got more
than the man with the rough voice and whiskey breath
who handed her hard ends of bread.
That's over now, Momma promises,
and A'Lelia believes her.
Folks come and go, but we always have each other.

UNBRAIDING

Momma unwinds A'Lelia's complicated braids.
After she blows out the lamp, walls creak,
laughter wails from the streets.
Even small sounds from her own body
keep A'Lelia awake.
She conjures a hero with eyes and skin
brown as the Mississippi riverbanks.
If her father were alive,
would they keep moving from Walnut to Clark Street,
past Union Station, farther from the church,
in search of a cheap, safe home?
Would they have two or three rooms instead of one
that smells of lye soap so strong it stings skin?
She knows only that he was tall.

She hugs her soft cloth doll and asks for another story
about the girl whose father disappeared
when he was needed. Cinderella has long, thick hair,
glistening eyes, and strong brown arms
that she plunges into pails.
With no books in this home, the only pictures
are those A'Lelia conjures.
A palace is the white house her mother says

stood on a hill by the cotton plantation.
What girl doesn't love the ending
when a glass slipper fits?
The fairy godmother is forgotten
as a prince brings happily ever after.

THE GAME

In the small steamy room, Momma scrubs petticoats,
dresses, and cotton shirts of strangers
who live across the tracks.
She squeezes water from fabric, twists pain to pride.

A'Lelia says, *When I grow up,*
we'll live in a castle.

Honey, there aren't castles in St. Louis.

Then we'll buy a big house. What color walls?

I don't care about the color, but I like lots of windows.
And why not marble pillars in front?
And crystal chandeliers.
Momma pulls a dress out of water tinged pink
from the red-brown earth. She croons gospel songs,
bleaches, pins, folds, lugs,
asks, *What kind of gowns should we wear?*
Green velvet, blue silk, or brocade?
Do you like emeralds or rubies?

Silver or gold?

A'Lelia twirls so fast the room becomes a ballroom.
Someday I'll find you a castle.

On Porch Steps

Momma pockets coins, says, *Thank you, ma'am.*
Have a good day, Mrs. Myrtle.

I'll see you next week, Sarah, the lady replies,
taking the basket.

Walking away, A'Lelia asks, *Why do you call her Mrs.*
while she uses your first name?

It's just the way it is.

A'Lelia feels the weight of stacked sheets
she no longer holds. There are two sides of town
back and front doors
those who can enter both and
those who'd better knock on just one.
Everything can be divided.
Black or white, light or dark, straight or nappy.

They turn a corner, pass their church where the choir
rehearses songs of rivers, roads, and rain.
The congregation is also split.
Women wearing elegant hats
are invited to the choir.
Women like Momma sing in the back.

AT THIRTEEN

A'Lelia catches her breath as her mother
lifts her calico bandanna.
Momma has lost enough hair
to show skin on the top of her head.
She kneels by the straw-filled mattress and murmurs,
Lord, thank you for another day,
our meals, our roof. Keep my girl safe.

How can she stand to pray the same thing
over and over?
A'Lelia wonders. Why won't she ask for more?
The prayer pinches, small as the jar under the mattress
holding coins so A'Lelia can go to a better school,
can one day find work far from farms
or white people's laundry, dishes, kitchen floors,
nurseries where children play or cry.
Someday, Momma promises,
she might even get piano lessons.

Why can't this life be enough?
A'Lelia brushes and braids her own hair,
no longer has reason to lean against her mother,
forgets the scent of her skin. She wishes
her mother would dump the old nickels and dimes,

buy herself a hat with silk roses and plumes.
She's sick of hearing about backs, bearing, and bending,
sad songs A'Lelia will not sing.

Momma rolls off her knees onto the mattress
they share, touches her wispy hair. *It can't grow*
on what food we can afford. I don't suppose
you remember when my hair was stronger?

A'Lelia's throat tightens with *Sorry.*
Instead, she says, *I don't remember.*

Momma turns away, rubs in Queen Pomade,
La Creole Hair Restorer, and Kinkilla.
Still, more hair laces the hot sheets.
Every night she prays
like a girl who goes to dances, hoping for a partner
though no one takes her hand.

PIECES

For you, Momma says,
handing A'Lelia a plaid dress.
Her face shines with too much hope
for what is secondhand, though washed,
pressed, cradled in her arms.
A'Lelia watches her mother lean
back over a laundry tub.
How can she bear to be the girl
who demands such giving up?
She snaps, *I never liked plaid.*

Where did this voice, tight as a fist, come from?
When did she become a shop with a sign:
Closed. Sold out?
Once, happiness was hers always. These days
gloom seeps through the alleys of her bones.
The blanket that kept her warm
turns shoddy overnight.
She steps back from her own body
as if pieces of her clatter to the floor—
arms, neck, back, hair—as if she became
a beggar, a lunatic,
an invader holding a gun.

MORNING AFTER MORNING

God leaves no footprints in the house.
Momma sighs as she plucks wrinkled blouses
from the floor, says,
Can't you put anything where it belongs?

A'Lelia says, *I like my clothes there
where I can see them.*

What are you doing still in bed?

Momma, it's Saturday.

*And I've got wash to deliver.
I don't suppose you'll help.*

That night A'Lelia meets a boy on the corner.
Later, Momma scolds,
Are you ashamed to ask him to our home?

Yes. A'Lelia slips on her nightgown.
She drops her dress by a jam jar
filled with wisteria and warm water
tinged brown from stalks.
Momma widens her eyes, closes them,
prays: *Please, Lord, let me keep my hair.*

A'Lelia wonders, Is this the first time
her mother has asked
for something just for herself?
The air shifts.
Maybe God notices, too.

Telling Fortunes

A'Lelia's heart beats so hard it wakes her.
Before she can murmur *yes* or *no*
to the boy who crept through
her sleep, before she crosses fully to waking,
Momma ladles out grits. She says,
Last night I had a dream.
She describes, almost shyly, an African savanna.
Sweet-smelling plants had blossoms
the color of cornbread.

A'Lelia shrugs. She leaves for school to study
geography, grammar, verse, sewing, and elocution.
She can't wait to walk with a boy
by the slow river.

When she gets home, she finds herbs on the table:
lavender, burdock root, rose hips, elder flowers.
Momma went to the pharmacy, too,
for small jars of tetter salve, petrolatum,
copper sulfate. Wax from bees. She offers a whiff
of sweet coconut oil. *From palm trees in Africa.*
The recipe came from my dream.
She mixes a concoction,
spreads it over her broken hair.

A'Lelia bends over a dish of mashed blossoms
like the woman who peers into emptied cups and
finds hints of the future in dried tea leaves.
The scents of herbs from far-flung places
remind both daughter and mother
that the world is bigger than this city.

INVENTED MIRRORS

All day, water laps Momma's elbows
as she holds a washboard steady. At night,
she becomes a chemist, the kitchen a laboratory
that smells like a dark forest. As her hair grows
longer, stronger, thicker, she leaves home more.
The tall woman stands taller at church.
She dines with the handsome C. J. Walker:
An educated man!
He not only reads newspapers, he writes for them.

Momma, he sells advertisements for the Clarion.

He smells of mint
and the pomade he slicks on his mustache.
He is not like the man who gave A'Lelia
heels of bread and sent her to the corner
before blowing out lamps,
but romance takes up too much room
in their small home.
A'Lelia is almost grown, but she misses the way
her mother gathered and lathered her hair,
toweled it dry,
rested her hands on her head.
Like the last pieces of a puzzle, everything fits together:

the girl she is at school, the girl she is with a boy,
the girl she is at home.

Momma hands A'Lelia a brochure
from a school where
she can train to be a teacher.

Why would I want to spend my life in a classroom?

You'd rather do laundry? Clean kitchens?

There must be other choices.
When her mother plans a new life
with kin who went to Denver for better jobs,
A'Lelia heads another way.

TRADING PLACES

On the train heading west, Momma looks away
as she passes fields where barbs clutch soft cotton bolls.
A vendor balances a tray with sandwiches and fruit.
Momma points to an apple. *How much?*
She shakes her head at the price,
but supposes it's better
than trying the dining car,
which might be reserved
for white folks. She makes do
with an apple, tears the skin with her teeth.
A yellow jacket claims the core.

Across the aisle, a grandmother tells stories
to children by her knees.
A younger woman rests her head on the window.
Her lap holds a toddler and a baby
whose brown elbow is slung over her ear.
She hushes a small boy who wails *I'm hungry.*
Another woman tilts her neck for a man's attention.
Momma signals the conductor, asks him
to send a roast chicken and loaf of bread
to the woman with three children.
She whispers, *Make sure the bread is good.*
Send the bill to me.

AWAY

Everyone here knows everybody else,
A'Lelia is certain.
The other girls know where they are going.
In Knoxville, Tennessee,
no one cares what A'Lelia has for lunch
or if she leaves clothing on the floor.
Only teachers notice
if she is late for class. Her head is untouched
until she meets a slim musician
who carries most of his weight in his shoulders.
His elbows sway as he blows into a trombone.
Breath gusting through brass
turns to music.

Then he finds another girl. A'Lelia sits on a rock
hears cicadas: *ch-chu-chrrrr, ch-chu-chrrr.*
Had the insects been crying or praying or whatever
they were doing all day, all fall?
Had she only heard now?

A shabby room, a castle, college: particular places
don't matter. She just doesn't want to live
where she can't hear the world around her. She
can't wait for a letter, splurges on a telegram.
Momma, I'm coming home.

Wonderful Hair Grower

A'Lelia's mother, aunt, and cousins stir
pots as big as laundry tubs.
A'Lelia helps bring potions
to kitchens around Denver.
They say *strengthen* and *smooth*, not *straighten*,
ask women, *Which side do you part your hair on?*
After they point, A'Lelia suggests,
Let's try the other side. Hey, that changes everything!

Momma does only her own wash now.
She gently rubs cleansers and conditioners
into the hair of women glad to sit and spill secrets.
She moves her hands in circles, casts a spell
over women who trust their heads to her hands.
Is the water warm enough? Too hot?
Women coo with the pleasure of being asked
what they want.

A'Lelia heats a metal comb on a stove
pulls it through hair with creams
that soften and shine.
Her smile is bright as a mirror
that can hold a whole person at a time
as she says, *Oh, my!* and means it.

When there's more work than mother, daughter,
aunt, and cousins can handle, Momma writes
to Mr. C. J. Walker. He gives up his newspaper job
and joins them, taking mail orders
for the Wonderful Hair Grower and other products.
He and Momma marry.

Happily, she puts pictures of herself in advertisements.
The woman who said *Yes, missus, yes, ma'am*
too many times
now says *Call me madam, Madam C. J. Walker.*
Glamour, dignity, power: She claims it all.

COSTUME

Momma lectures in parlors and church basements.
She holds her back straight
as she speaks about wanting, will, and work.
Her eyes stay steady on the ladies in the back
as she says *The vision was a gift.*

Does she pretend triumph is an accident,
afraid a prize displayed too boldly
might be snatched away?
Modesty is her disguise. Never mind.
Women want to know not only the ingredients
of Walker hair treatments—
lavender, burdock root, sulfur—
but the story behind them:
A washerwoman puts away her tubs.
Anyone can change her life.

TRAVELING

On sales trips through Colorado
Kansas
Oklahoma
Texas
and Arkansas
A'Lelia, Sarah, and C. J. Walker rent rooms
in boarding houses or hotels.
Momma stoops to pluck stockings off the floor.
A'Lelia takes a lavender gown
from her densely packed trunk.
Momma, sit down. The maid will clean.

Momma unbends with visible effort,
pulls back her hands.
She hires dressmakers to stitch
exquisite holes for silver buttons,
loves watching numbers unwind and expand
across paper, but as years pass, can she recognize
the fortune slowly being built
as they train women
to sell products door to door?
The Walker agents, wearing neat black skirts
and starched white blouses, leave jobs

in white women's kitchens, nurseries,
and laundry rooms.
Colored women speak to colored women:
How can I help you? May I have the pleasure?
A wish, long-treasured, becomes a magic wand.

HEIRESS

A'Lelia chooses dresses with gold lace and velvet cuffs,
lovelier than gowns her mother used to wash.
She buys apple-green slippers, silver bangles,
and for her shelves, miniature elephants:
jade, ivory, and ebony. In shops,
she points to crystal flasks of perfume,
ostrich feather fans, opera glasses, and
coats with fur collars and cuffs. Gifts for her mother
include rose-scented hand creams,
black pearls, jade bowls,
an opal brooch circled with diamonds.

Momma thanks her, then waves big bills.
What in heaven's name were you thinking?

We're not poor anymore.

All you do is spend.

Who will listen to you talk
about beauty if your dress is last season's?

One can slide between poor and rich,
the difference as slight as between
paper and parchment

one voice and a choir
arms hanging by sides and a hug.
A'Lelia coaxes Momma to an elegant shop where
they touch a silk blouse. Pearl buttons
are artfully hidden in a froth of fabric
that ripples like thick cream.
Its sleeves cross, then unfold
like a gorgeous conversation.
It costs a small fortune.

Imagine it wrapped
in tissue paper in a glossy box.

MISSING

A Walker salon and factory is built in Indianapolis.
As years pass, the skin near Momma's mouth puckers.
She rubs her neck and temples. *I haven't felt well.*
My doctor gave me medicine, but says I need rest, too.

You can afford to go to a warm beach.
Take your husband.

Momma won't speak of the man who now works
hundreds of miles away.
She protests, *There's too much work.*

Go to Europe. Buy gowns in Paris. See those castles
we used to dream about.
A'Lelia eats caviar, sips champagne.
Why can't her mother forget
the taste of half-spoiled potatoes?
She dodges holidays as if just a few days off
may make her stumble back
to years of washtubs.

How can I rest when there's so much to be done?
Momma's shoulders bend as she hears reports
of colored men hanged from trees. She gives
to good causes as well as to aunts, cousins, neighbors.

Some offer thanks. Some ask for more.
Momma braces against whispers
from those certain they'd use the fortune more wisely.
She says, *Sometimes I miss our old days.*

Washing clothes? Momma, you don't.

ELEVATOR, PITTSBURGH, PENNSYLVANIA

In the driver's seat of a shiny black motorcar
A'Lelia blasts past horses pulling buggies.
She parks and enters a hotel elevator.

Going up? The attendant's voice melts
like chocolate in sun.

Yes, please.

The tall young man with hard shoulders and
round brown eyes snaps shut the accordion gate.
A'Lelia's belly lurches as the elevator swings up.

As she steps out, the handsome
man says, *Have a good day, miss.*

His voice plunges to parts of A'Lelia's body
she never learned to name. She turns from the hip,
says, *Think I'll go back down.*

That evening, they leave a fine restaurant,
his fingertips on the small of her back. Another night,
John Robinson takes her hand.
Walls, roofs, and roads disappear.

CONVERSATION

Snow falls on iron fences. Ice slicks sidewalks.
A'Lelia and John enter a shop
where a tailor shows them soft woolens,
measures John's shoulders, back, and legs.
A'Lelia asks that the bill
be sent to her mother's accountant.

The amount and address don't go unnoticed.

What's this? You're buying suit jackets and trousers?

A'Lelia is silent. Momma asks, *What will folks say?*
Your Mr. Robinson runs an elevator.

You did laundry. Did that make you less of a person?

I didn't go after someone else's hard-earned money.

You don't know him. He's a good man.

But not very ambitious.

Momma, you're driven enough for us all.

Momma's hands spread
the way they once did at the grocer's
weighing a cabbage: *Can we afford it?*

Instead, she points to plans to expand the company.

I'm thinking of your future.

Though I suppose it's getting near time

for you to have a baby.

Someone to watch over our business one day.

Business! Is that all you think about?

Momma doesn't answer. She packs her bags.

ONE YEAR OF HER LIFE

A'Lelia chooses a silver-green dress
with French lace
at the collar, long amber beads. Strangers witness
as she marries John Robinson in the courthouse.

That night, drawing the curtains, she looks out.
Stars flicker in the turning-black sky. Traffic
rumbles in the street. She pulls the curtain
tighter. Laughter and kisses
make her feel split, then whole.

After the honeymoon, most mornings
John tucks a gold shoehorn into the boots
a maid polishes.
He chooses jackets and trousers of wool
so finely woven they slide under A'Lelia's hands.
He looks for a new job
while she measures ingredients,
stirs new formulas, trains beauticians.

One evening, a yellow and black dog,
his skinny back bent,
sniffs by their door. John raises his hand,
shouts, *What are you doing here? Get out!*

She says, *The poor dog must be hungry.*

Don't you dare sass me! John lifts his hand again,
then takes his hard voice outside.
When he comes back, supper is cold.
He makes promises. His arms
around her put broken pieces
together. His voice takes back its old music.
She kisses him, but one morning claims,
My mother misses me. I'll be back soon.
She won't call this place home.

WAITING FOR MUSIC

A city block of buildings in Indianapolis
all bearing the Walker name:
a factory, offices, and a salon where colored women
have good jobs. Momma offers prizes
first for those who make the most sales,
then for those who give the most to charity.

One night she decides to see a movie.
At the Isis Theatre she is asked
for twenty-five cents while
white folks are charged a dime.
Rage makes Madam Walker stand tall.
She sends lawyers to set things straight.
She calls an architect to have a movie palace
built beside the Walker company
where colored people are welcomed.

A'Lelia visits to help with plans.
One night, taking potatoes off the stove,
A'Lelia says, *Look at all you've done.*

Momma sips tomato juice, says, *It's over.*
A'Lelia knows she means her marriage.
She hasn't seen C. J. in months.

He'll keep a share in the business.
I'll keep the name.

A'Lelia pours hot water into the sink,
watches it spiral down the drain. She goes to the hall,
sets the needle on the pale blue Victrola.
A record spins out the blues. Flattened notes slide
into longing. There can be no music without stopping,
without pauses between notes.

Steps

A'Lelia returns to Philadelphia.
Her husband doesn't meet her train
or greet her at the door. She opens her suitcase,
arranges her small elephants on the bureau,
puts away silk blouses, then sees
John's soft tailored clothes are gone.

She yanks out empty drawers,
lets them crash. She throws open the closet door.
Only a shoehorn glimmers in a dark corner.
She bends over to snatch it.
Glass slippers can't be forced to fit.
She flings the gold shoehorn across the room.
Miniature elephants scatter—
jade, ivory, ebony—collide into walls.
Why had she thought she needed them?
What good had they done?

At last she goes to the kitchen,
tears chicken from a bone.
She sets out the tender dark meat
and sits on a step, arms around her knees,
certain the yellow and black dog will come back.

Mae, Thirteen

Salon mirrors reflect rows of jars labeled
with pictures of Madam C. J. Walker.
Scissors flare open, snap shut.
Spoons swirl and clatter.
Water flows from tipped heads into porcelain:
benediction, a new chance. Women smooth and pin
until buoyant hair lies flat.

A girl with a thick braid to her waist runs in.
A'Lelia hands her a broom. *You're late.*
Were you kept at school?

I stopped going. My mother needs the money
I make here.
My sisters and brothers have got to eat.

A'Lelia plucks a yellow flower from a vase
and tucks it behind Mae's ear. After a year of seeing
the wide-eyed girl work hard, A'Lelia
invites her home, gives her velvet and lace
cast-off dresses.
How can Mae leave her very own canopy bed,
orange slices on blue plates for breakfast,
for a room where four children share one mattress?

A'Lelia arranges an adoption, offering luxuries
and an education Mae's mother can't afford.
Why shouldn't you have more
than I ever thought possible?
One day we'll see a bit of the world.
Moats. Turrets. Towers.

On pink satin sheets, Mae weeps at night,
but what thirteen-year-old girl doesn't cry in the dark?

HARLEM

Europe's castles must wait, but A'Lelia and Mae visit
studios crowded with canvases, paints,
daisies stashed in bottles drained of cheap wine.
A'Lelia finds a cobbler who makes magnificent shoes,
then walks past brownstone buildings.
Girls with skinny legs wear socks
with neatly folded cuffs.
They jump over spinning ropes.
Boys catch or chase balls.
Music rises through cracks in the Harlem sidewalks
into the soles of A'Lelia's feet,
to her hips and shoulders.

For supper, she finds a place on Seventh Avenue
where linen napkins are folded into fans.
A man dips his back and raises a trombone.
Bold, brassy sounds hold back the dark. A woman
steps onstage to sing about where a girl has been
and where she dreams of going.
Her voice is like church and chocolate cake
and crying.
Just the right amount of sugar nudges
loneliness from nights. Saxophones and bass viols

urge high steps across streets
she and Momma once crossed carrying laundry.
The world at last stops splitting.
A'Lelia wants to live where she,
though almost six feet tall,
can wear high heels, where anyone can be beautiful.
We'll open a shop.

She chooses a four-story townhouse.
On the first floor, the walls of the Walker Hair Salon
are painted pearl gray.
A'Lelia buys marble-topped tables.
Beaded curtains open to a garden and gazebo.
Soon women whisk lotions, wash hair, whisper secrets.
Clients put down newspapers, sometimes argue:
Why send soldiers overseas
when problems right here aren't fixed?
A'Lelia hears hope in her tapping hammer as she hangs
bold paintings on the walls of apartments she lavishly
furnishes above the hair salon. She buys
Mae a gold piano, hires a woman to give her lessons.
A'Lelia's elbows grow stiff with waiting to applaud.

Most mornings, she picks up blouses by Mae's bed.
I don't spend good money
so you can drop clothes on the floor.

Mae shrugs.

A'Lelia opens a letter from her mother,
who isn't well and begs her only child to visit.

No, she writes back. *Momma, come to New York.*

River View

Madam Walker chooses a view of the Hudson River
and millionaire neighbors
named Rockefeller and Vanderbilt.
Her mansion has thirty rooms, white pillars
around the porch, and curved balconies
overlooking close-clipped grass and rose beds.
It's bigger than the house of the family
who owned cotton fields
and claimed to own her parents, too.
The house is her way to say *times change.*

Of course A'Lelia meant *Come to Harlem,*
not up the river, dragging old dreams and nightmares.
What use are white pillars?
A'Lelia doesn't miss where she grew up
sharing one cupboard, a mattress, and a washtub,
but there are choices beyond this sweep of green lawn.
Still, she helps Momma fill crystal vases with tulips,
stacks shelves with leather-bound books
no one will read.
Momma won't light the expensive stove in the kitchen,
but each object pushes back the past she can't bear
to remember. She rubs her forehead

as if she might erase lines made by the war in Europe,
while at home men are lynched, women violated,
children go hungry. She writes checks to charities
and people who promise change, swallows
aspirin with ginger ale. She wanders
to the window in her stocking feet, gazes at the river,
more winding and sparkling
than the old view of the Mississippi.

A'Lelia orders a long mahogany table—
It's perfect for parties—
to celebrate not only her mother's success,
but that of every woman
who did laundry or washed dishes for others
and stopped.

Doors

A'Lelia and her mother raise money for hospitals
that take in soldiers
wounded in England and France.
A'Lelia drives Momma
to the Red Cross office to volunteer.
One white woman looks at another,
holds silence too long.
Momma straightens her back, stiff as ice, and turns.
Since *our women* are barred from the Red Cross,
she helps start the Circle for Negro War Relief.
Don't wait for an open door, she says.
Open one yourself.

A'Lelia drives an ambulance carrying the disabled
and dangerously ill to New York hospitals.
In the evenings, she dances with new friends
who go to bed at dawn.
Twenty-four gold bracelets jangle on her wrist.
Sometimes she visits her mother,
though it's hard to sleep
in the perfect white house
with too many servants,
their footsteps too quietly placed.

She hears her mother get up for a glass of water,
switch on the lamp on her desk,
open ledger books and go over accounts
she paid someone to audit,
as if she can't believe her good fortune.

OPEN HOUSE

When the Great War ends, A'Lelia joins
the Colored Women's Motor Corps in a parade
to welcome home soldiers.
Horns honk, bells clang, whistles blare.
Children bang on cookie tins,
toss candy and coins,
fling caps above red-and-blue bunting.
Men of the all-black 369th Infantry Regiment,
rifles slung on shoulders,
or beating drums, march up Fifth Avenue.
Soldiers keep step until they cross into Harlem,
where they break out of line and shout.
Home at last!

Momma invites veterans to her mansion,
holding the door open
as if she were born for this moment.
Young men with arms in slings or bandaged heads sip
from crystal goblets.
One leans on crutches, making his way
across the Persian carpet to the portico,
down marble steps for a view
of rose gardens and the river.

A'Lelia makes small talk
and flirts under the hand-painted ceiling.
She passes around drinks
then leaves the party to maids and guests.
She finds her mother poring over calendars,
numbers, and notes. Her hands are rough from years
of soap too strong for lotion to salve.

Momma, you've worked your whole life.
Let's celebrate your fiftieth birthday in Europe.

Maybe next year. Right now I need
you to work on sales in Cuba.

The Caribbean beaches will be warm. Why
don't you come, too? Relax, like your doctor orders.

Not now.

A'Lelia kisses her cheek, so soft
it crumples under her lips.

Turquoise Sea

Waves splash, spatter, pull back, spill,
and retreat to the sea, sounding like soiled clothes
dragged up and sloshed back down
into dirty water. A'Lelia ducks, so waves crash
on her shoulders. Mae hands her a towel, then they
plan sales meetings
while waiting for a cool breeze.
They play cards under a cabana,
spread guava jam on toast,
eat mango slices and coconut cake.

A'Lelia strolls on white sand. Brown-skinned women
holding babies bend to children tugging their skirts.
Their hair is beautifully braided
glistens with coconut oil
or is wrapped in bright bandannas.
What has she got to sell to them?
When a girl holds out her open palm,
A'Lelia fills it with coins, grateful
for the way she looks her straight in the eye.

CIRCLES

After A'Lelia gets the telegram, she dives
under warm waves where she can't hear whispers.
She books passage on a ship. Once in New Orleans,
she learns that her mother's heart is failing fast.
She boards a train, hears wheels
spin on the track. *Hurry, hurry.*

It's too late. She missed
the dying, misses the funeral.
The choir has gone home,
but she's crowded by consolation:
Your mother was so good, so generous.
The Walker saleswomen insist. *She changed our lives.*

The casket is left for her to view, the bronze lid open.
Her mother's hands are folded together, her elegant
neck exposed. Nothing is hidden now,
and nothing will be known
but what she knows already.
A'Lelia drops roses on the casket. All the arguments
are over. Who's spoiled, who's proud, who works hard,
who doesn't care enough: What use had they been?
No voice lingers like the one she longs to hear
slow as the Mississippi River sloshing grief

on its banks. Why had she ever before
thought she was alone?
She knows the word's meaning now.

She doesn't want to sort pretty things, to choose
among memories that fall too hard
as she picks up gold rings
or photographs in filigree frames. She has enough,
she always had enough.
She shuts the wide white door
and locks it. It was never the house she loved
but the woman no longer inside.

TOURIST

A'Lelia takes Mae to Paris shops, touches ornaments
her mother might like, then remembers.
She and Mae swim in the Riviera,
see a new pope crowned in Rome,
ride camels in Egyptian deserts,
watch opera in London.
A'Lelia buys tickets to tour castles where no one lives.
Her shoes *click-clack* in ballrooms, where she wonders
what kind of music was once played.
Women bend to girls
and whisper, *Which do you like more,*
rubies or emeralds?

Sick of hair and debates
about how a woman should wear it,
A'Lelia covers hers with a turban now.
Was Europe her mother's dream or hers?
She can't remember. From the hotel window
she sees a dog by a wrought-iron gate who seems
to wait for no one. She spends the afternoon
making calls: Where does the pretty dog belong?
Why doesn't she have a home?
A'Lelia draws the curtain.

The past isn't a rock she can walk away from;
it stays with her, sometimes invisible, sometimes small,
sometimes looming larger
than what's beneath her feet.
She knows that a girl who once did laundry
changed. Anyone can change.
Her mother is telling her stories still.

THE DARK TOWER

Back in Harlem, A'Lelia leaves the salon and climbs
the blue-carpeted stairs to the third floor
of the townhouse.
A silver punch bowl shines on the red table
in a room a poet calls the Dark Tower.
Above a skyscraper-shaped bookcase
poems are stenciled on the walls. "The Weary Blues"
hovers by paintings of buildings that look both broken
and alive: steeples lean, steps stagger.

A'Lelia sends invitations to more guests
than can possibly fit here.
She waves her hand as if casting
fairy dust, glitter: A castle needn't have turrets.
Strangers and friends mingle
with Broadway stars, sculptors, bankers, painters,
and people determined to brighten their walls,
rich folk and those without a dime.
A parrot squawks, "Hello!"

Trumpets and tubas mark
the strong beats, weak beats, and off beats of jazz.
Heads nod, hands clap, feet tap to the rhythm of
lingering chords

long blue notes
breaks and riffs.
Roll the bass.
Skip and miss.
Slur and slide.

Princes and poor women
dance the Lindy Hop, Charleston, jitterbug.

Dresses are narrower and shorter
than they were last year.
Many women wear their hair shorter, too.
Will the Walker business falter? Who can tell?
Style is a swift dash, fashions unfurl fast as
loops of pearls swinging from A'Lelia's throat.
Fringe flutters from her gold-beaded dress
while guests talk about color and line, clay
and bronze, choose art to buy. Beneath chandeliers,
they admire canvases of gray-eyed grief
dressed in a shabby sweater and torn skirts,
or women with all kinds of hair, all beautiful.

Paint, A'Lelia urges her friends, night after night. *Write.*
She applauds poets who claim every possible word
and thousands of ways to arrange them.
Take to the stage, she says. *Dance. Sing.*

Make music. Many pick up trumpets, tap drums,
let jazz blur lines between
sorrow songs and jubilees,
pull together the split world. Nothing is divided.
Perhaps white can be black, black can turn white,
boys can be girls, and girls may be boys.

Jazz never ends but circles
until broken pieces of A'Lelia
come together. Bass notes
call up her old home where the Mississippi
laps brown earth and strong arms pick cotton
or plunge into wash and water.
Drums own the past, rapping
not to glorify old work but the worker,
the one who stood it, with few choices—
and pound new paths
toward places no one has yet traveled,
lands of lost slippers
where at last everyone
finds a perfect fit.

LEGACIES

MADAM C. J. WALKER is recognized as an entrepreneur who generously contributed to organizations, particularly those promoting opportunity and justice for people of color. Her will included her wish that there should always be a woman heading the Madam C. J. Walker Manufacturing Company.

After her death in 1919, her daughter helped run the business, though A'Lelia Walker is remembered most for the way she often opened her home to singers, musicians, writers, artists, and their patrons, making it a vital part of the creative period known as the Harlem Renaissance.

A'Lelia died of a cerebral hemorrhage in 1931. Her

funeral was by invitation only, but newspapers reported that more than ten thousand people crowded New York City's Seventh Avenue, hoping for a glimpse of the orchids on her silver casket. Her adopted daughter, Mae, inherited a share of the company and A'Lelia's townhouse at 108–110 West 136th Street, which eventually was torn down. A branch of the New York Public Library, famous for its collection of African-American history, was built in its place.

Descendants continued to work at the Madam C. J. Walker Manufacturing Company until it was sold in 1986. The theater at the Indianapolis, Indiana, site remains open as a performing arts center and includes a small Walker museum. Madam C. J. Walker's great-great-granddaughter, A'Lelia Bundles, became an award-winning producer for ABC and NBC and a writer. Her biographies of her ancestors keep their memories alive.

IRÈNE JOLIOT-CURIE AND MARIE CURIE

MARIE CURIE
AND
IRÈNE JOLIOT-CURIE

INVISIBLE FORCES

AFTER HER MOTHER died of tuberculosis, ten-year-old Marie Sklodowska counted rosary beads, but prayer brought little consolation. She missed her mother. Wishing desperately for a chance to make her proud, she concentrated on her schoolwork.

At seventeen, Marie left Warsaw to teach in another part of Poland. When she'd saved some money, she followed her sister, Bronya, to France, where women could study advanced science. In Paris, Marie met a tall professor with long pale hands, a rough brown beard, and wrinkles framing his blue eyes. She and Pierre Curie sipped hot tea and spilled numbers across a pine table, trying to comprehend the forces inside an atom.

They fell in love, though Marie was worried: She hadn't planned to stay in France. Pierre promised to learn Polish so she wouldn't be homesick. For a simple wedding ceremony in the town hall, Marie chose a dark woolen jacket and skirt she could wear later in the laboratory. The two scientists didn't exchange rings, since Marie didn't want to bother taking one off to work.

Their daughter Irène Curie was born in 1897, two years after the wedding. She was seven years old and green eyed with a blond fluff of hair that was turning brown when her sister Eve was born.

RUN

Ducking as if under rain,
Irène scrambles beside her mother,
who drops one arm to lift her little sister.
Eve squeals and kicks, missing the ground.
Their mother's other arm curves, an umbrella
over Irène until they reach the garden next door.
Irène steps out toward her friend Aline.
The girls, both serious, loyal,
and nine years old, climb the rock they call a castle.

Mé, which is what the girls call their mother,
presses Eve into the arms of Aline's mother.
She smooths the small girl's smock over her diaper
and leans into her friend
for a squall of whispers.
Mé's eyes are gray as the tree trunks in forests
of fairy tales she refuses to tell.

Irène leaps from the rock, waves a green net
over the small and important kingdom. She snaps
down her arm, scoops out her prey. Eve touches
the velvety edge of a wing, an intricate antenna.
They count four wings, one slightly ripped, and six legs.
Eve says, *Mine.*

Irène turns. Their mother has gone.
Never mind. She knows what she'd say:
The butterfly is alive.
We must let her go.

Eve wails. Irène scolds her.
Is this why Mé silently left,
sick of a small girl's noise?
But as the butterfly escapes,
Irène soothes her sister. Who can help wanting
the flutter of soft wings between her hands?

First Night

Your mother says you're to stay here tonight.
Aline's mother picks up blue-eyed, black-haired Eve.
Irène wonders why
their mother didn't tell them herself
as she and Aline follow to the kitchen. Spare chairs
are already around the table, unlike at home,
where five straw-bottomed chairs are just enough
for Irène, her mother, father, sister, and grandfather.

The kitchen smells of chicken, potatoes,
and pale yellow cakes shaped like shells.
After supper, Monsieur Perrin
tells Eve stories about girls in gorgeous dresses
who get lost in forests or lose glass slippers.
Once his wife takes Eve upstairs, Monsieur Perrin,
a scientist, like Irène's parents,
writes equations for the older girls to solve.
When Irène falters, she looks back
to see where she made a mistake.

Soon she climbs to the bedroom where Eve kneels,
chubby hands clasped. Madame Perrin chants words
banished from their house, like carpets or curtains
that need cleaning or block views.

Eve is too young to know
the Curies prize investigation over certainty.
Irène knows,
but wonders if prayer could hush the *tha-thum*
too high in her chest.
Mé has said she must decide for herself
whether or not to enter cathedrals. But living
in a house stripped to essentials, where Mé owns only
two black dresses, one to be worn while the other
is laundered, how can she choose
the clutter of steeples, stained glass, and statues?
How can she pray when Mé and Papa
pare even words,
often skipping *hello* and *good-bye?*
A face or a back is sufficient.

Madame Perrin pulls down the covers of the bed
Eve and Irène will share. After she leaves—
when no one leans to kiss good night
no blue light flashes from Papa's pocket—
the sisters tiptoe to the window. Across the yard,
their home shines with blocks of yellow-gold light.
Are the strangers at the door holding slim notebooks
and bulky cameras reporters?
Will Mé send them away,

rather than waste her time
with questions that already have answers?

Eve asks, *What's wrong?*

Everything is fine.
This is a big sister's script.
She sends Eve back to bed.
Did Mé and Papa win another gold medal
to tuck in a bureau behind socks, since nothing
on a mantel means nothing to be dusted?
She remembers them taking a train to Sweden
where a woman might earn the Nobel Prize
but would be kept from speaking on the stage.

Irène slips under the covers, pushes Eve's head
to the pillow's side.
Pressing her cheek on the warm spot
Eve left, she imagines a woman
claiming a place at the podium.
Scientists, gentlemen, ladies, I have something to say.

BETWEEN GARDENS

Midmorning, Mé crosses the yard
carrying clean clothes.

Eve slams into her, shouting,
I didn't say good night!

I wanted to check that your hair got combed.
You both ate breakfast? You're minding Madame Perrin?

Of course, Mé, Irène says. *Where's Papa?*

Mé rubs the split skin on her fingertips.
He doesn't feel well.

He needs me to pat his sore legs, Irène says.
Who will remind him to tie his shoes
or sip the coffee
he stirs too long? *I have to feed the cat.*

Not now. Mé's eyes look more like Papa's,
clouded with daydream. She turns back to the house,
where horses stamp in front of still carriages.

Eve shrieks.

Hush. Mé has to work. Irène hands her a stick.
Let's play being Mother.

Eve's tears dry as she winds the branch through air
like a woman stirring a pot of boiling ore.
Before Eve was born,
Mé emptied sacks of pitchblende raked from a forest
plucked broken pine needles from the brown powder
set the dark ore in a pot over a fire, stirred
with an iron rod. She boiled, dissolved,
boiled, cooled, rinsed, and boiled again
until crystals formed, proof
that what cannot be seen has power.

Mé and Papa spent years in the glass-roofed shed
that stores lumber and old equipment
as well as experiments.
The pinewood table turned radioactive
before Mé created the word.
Irène hates the dirt floor, the cracked windows.
It's hot in summer and cold in winter. But one night she
begged to see the pale blue glow from bowls of crystals
light the room under the leaking roof.

Irène nudged between her parents as they stared
the way she is certain they once gazed at her.

WILD HORSES

On the third day at the neighbors',
under the gray sky,
Irène and Aline gallop on invisible horses,
whipping jump ropes as reins.
Eve tries to keep up.
Mé doesn't pass the roses, the place
where turtles nest by a rock, until afternoon.
Irène keeps her hands tight as if around reins
while Mé silences the world with her whisper.
A butterfly's cream-colored wings flit, fold,
open to flash red spots ringed with black.

Irène breaks away, gallops, trots, tosses her hair;
she is the horse, not the rider,
with no bridle or saddle.

She's too young to understand,
Mé murmurs to Madame Perrin.

No-no-no-no-no: Can a rope of words hold back
memories of Papa stirring his coffee, milk
swirling like earth circling sun? Irène looks back
the way she does at an equation to see where
she went wrong.

It is impossible that she'd play horses
if her father was dead, that her mother
would expect her curved arm to be safety,
combed hair a charm,
wait until he was buried to tell her.

BLACK UMBRELLA

Craving the scent of dust, Irène tucks up her knees
between the bed and desk covered with butterfly wings
on pins, still bright but useless, snail shells,
skins shed by snakes, jars of chloroform and cotton.
In the spare house, the only room that smells of
crumbling leather books, scavenged rocks,
dried flowers, and old medical charts
of organs and bones
belongs to her grandfather.

No one can see Irène as he says,
What was he dreaming of this time?

Grandpère tells a stranger
how his son opened his black umbrella in the street
crowded with women carrying long sticks of bread,
wagons of turnips or coal. Papa didn't see the horses,
dark with rain, until too late.
He tried to snatch the harness, took a wrong step
on slick stones, slipped under the wooden wheel.
The test tube of radium
he'd tucked in his pocket cracked.

SHE UNDERSTANDS

Irène calls the black-and-white cat
and cries when he won't come.

DOORS AND WINDOWS

Like a girl at a window listening to rain,
Irène holds her face against the door Mé shut.
Will the storm ever end? Downstairs, Grandpère
tells Eve the tale of a girl
with gold hair and glass slippers.
Memory presses too close on Mé,
while Irène's grandfather and sister
seem too light with forgetting.
I should have been with Papa.
I would have heard the horses, grabbed his hand.

Grandpère gets up to check the soup, skim froth
from the pudding on the stove. He calls Irène,
who won't come until Mé
opens the door.

After supper, Grandpère picks up an apple and knife.
Irène says, *Papa cut off the skin in spirals.*

Eve says, *I don't remember.*

Irène wants to slap her. Grandpère leaves on the peel,
slices the apple in quarters, carries dishes to the sink.
Mé plants her elbows on the table,
opens the diary she writes to Papa.

Irène says, *He can't read. He can't hear.*

I can't stop a conversation that went on so long.

She must stop! At last Mé opens her ordinary
clothbound notebooks with records of experiments,
recipes for gooseberry jam, and what is spent for milk,
grapes, eggs, the occasional pair of gloves or stockings.
Mé presses her hardened fingertips on her ears
and bends over her calculations
as she tries to pry out secrets
of the atom's wild invisible core.

Beside her, Irène spreads her schoolbooks on the table.
The salt shaker and cat and pot of geraniums
transform to numbers that her mind
curves around like a hand.
The room smells of sharp pencils,
with their snap like fall leaves, a dying campfire.
She is grateful for equations, which stubbornness
and thought can change.

ANOTHER SUMMER

Eve throws out her arms, demands an audience
as she sings, spins, swings the china doll
that Grandpère gave her. She piles thick mathematics
and medical books to perch on and play the piano.

She's too noisy! Irène shoves the cat from a chair
where radium has slipped unseen.

Mé opens a window, waves her stained hand
to fan sounds over the garden. *It's hot.*
In August, we'll go to the seashore.

Irène says, *Like we did with Papa.*

I don't remember. Eve sulks.

Maybe Irène understands.
Her memories are disappearing,
too, along with pieces of her grandfather:
first his eyesight, then his lap.
Only his smile remains as Irène brings roses
he can no longer tend, soup he can no longer stir.
Can he hear Eve pound black and white keys?

By the time Eve turns five, she knows thirty tunes.
Over and over she practices "Au Clair de la Lune"

and "La Marseillaise." She is playing that song again
when Mé shuts Grandpère's door,
puts an arm over Irène, and whispers.

No! Irène screams.

This time she insists on attending the burial.

Blue periwinkles, yellow irises grow near the open earth
by the grave of the man who tripped off the curb,
hands in his pockets,
mind too loud with numbers
to hear the whinny of horses,
wheels splitting on stones. Irène tightens her fist
around nothing that can be seen
the hands she can't hold.
She will never let go.

WITHOUT SCHOOL BELLS

Mé's mouth crumples
as she examines Irène's homework,
displeased with too-simple questions. She believes
Paris classrooms are too crowded. *Students waste weeks*
on subjects that can be learned in hours.
We can do better.

Mé hires two Polish girls to cook, clean, and tutor Eve.
She and other parents begin to teach
Irène, Aline Perrin, Isabelle Chavannes,
and seven other children.
Every Thursday it's Mé's turn.
She runs experiments with parabolas
or uses bricks, boards, and marbles to explain
the laws of falling bodies.
Isabelle yawns. Aline jabs her with an elbow.

On Fridays, Madame Perrin leads them
through the Louvre
or art galleries. She makes them memorize events
of reigns and revolutions. Irène likes her, but
she's happiest when Monsieur Langevin devotes
Mondays to mathematics, teaching geometry
with pins and string.

One afternoon, the black-haired physicist
explains that X-rays are like waves of visible light,
but too short and slim to see. Rays pass
through wood, cloth, tin, skin, and flesh.

Isabelle draws their teacher's profile in margins,
careful with the lovely line of his nose,
the curled tip of his waxed mustache.
Aline whispers to Irène,
You'd think she'd be embarrassed.
His children sit across the room.

Irène can't worry about yawns or crushes.
She needs to comprehend
the laws of radiance, reflection, refraction.
Every question and answer binds her
to the one world her mother loves.

IRÈNE, THIRTEEN

Slowly, grief lifts its gray net from the house.
Mé puts away black and irons white dresses,
astounds Irène with a rose at her sash. At supper
she asks silly questions about the day.
Irène says, *Remember how Papa used to stare at the sky?*
He talked about stars no one can see.

Eve says, *I don't remember.*

One day Mé asks Monsieur Langevin to help
hang a rope swing from the tree by the kitchen.
She drags out Papa's old bicycle and teaches
Irène how to mend the tires.
She shows Eve
how to lean to turn,
explains the torque of pedals,
the friction of slender wheels on gravel.

While Eve practices balance,
Irène watches a butterfly light on a leaf,
beat gold and purple wings four times,
then open them to glide. She cares less
for the butterflies' brilliance than the transparent hunger
that drives them between petals.

After supper, Irène says, *I can't wait to go to the ocean.*

I think, Mé says, *it's time for you girls*
to visit your Aunt Bronya.
You can work on your Polish.
Learn more about my homeland.

Eve asks, *Will you show us everything?*

Irène will look out for you, Mé says.
I can't leave my work.

Irène's heart beats too high in her chest.
She does not want to speak another language
every day, does not care to see her aunt and cousins,
to swim, ride horseback, trudge up mountains,
leave France or her friend Aline. She wants to hear
Ch-chu-chrrr as cicadas nibble bark from plane trees
and Monsieur Langevin talk about invisible rays.
Who will remind her mother to eat supper?
From another country, how can she be certain
Mé won't disappear?

ANOTHER COUNTRY

The black train winds past steep mountains
crosses invisible borders.
Eve clutches the doll Grandpère gave her
with its staring eyes in a china face but
assumes she'll find comfort in any country.
Minutes after meeting Aunt Bronya, Eve snuggles
by her side, nibbles poppy-seed cake, examines
her leather bag filled with doctor's instruments.

Irène finds nights too long here.
She waits for mail, solves mathematics problems
her mother sends, and writes, *Dear Mé,*
Has the cat escaped?
Is she fat? Are the peaches in the garden ripe?
Does my little palm tree have any new fronds?
Why didn't you come, too? Irène asks more questions,
which she numbers until she reaches ten.
She demands answers to them all.

GYMNASTICS CLASS

In September, Eve slams into Mé, crushing the red rose
pinned to her sash. Irène sees a flush to her skin
as she spreads plans for a new research center.
She is too busy now to teach. Other parents agree
the girls should now attend a regular school.
There, Irène and Aline whisper between wooden desks
about boys who dare to look at them;
should they look back?

Just before gymnastics class one afternoon,
Isabelle waves a newspaper.
Irène, didn't your mother show you
her picture on the front page?

Aline snatches the paper.
Madame Curie doesn't care about fame.

What does she care about?

Isabelle squishes her lips, smug, as if her mother,
silver cross by her throat, would not keep news from her.
Before she can say more,
Aline shoves Irène into the room
where they change clothes.
Soon the girls tumble on mats,

somersault, leap, swing from a trapeze
with ink-stained fingers.
Irène flings her body through the air.
The girls face one another and fall
in a game called trust.

Afterward, they wipe their warm foreheads
and change from bloomers back to dresses.
Irène wonders if her mother is so distracted
as to keep a discovery from her.
She picks up the newspaper Isabelle left by her shoes,
skims the headline.
Your mother acts like she's better than us,
Isabelle hisses. *She's not.*

Irène drops the paper, runs, Aline keeps up
past steps where folded newspapers wait,
too many for even a diligent daughter
to sweep away. All over Paris, newspapers rustle
in cafés. The name of the girls' former teacher
of mathematics and physics, Monsieur Langevin,
is linked with Mé's. A reporter wrote,
Shame on the Polish scientist
who tried to charm the husband
of a devout French wife.

Wheels screech, reins snap, someone shouts.
No-no-no-no-no: a firewall of words stops nothing.
Is this why her mother put away her black dresses
for white frocks and tucked roses into silk?
Why wasn't I with Papa on the slippery street
to pull him back from the shying horses?

Irène finds Mé in a friend's apartment
with Eve by her side. Arms round each other,
who holds up whom?
Let's go home, Irène begs. *Don't hide.*

Mé doesn't move.

Alone, Irène heads back to their house,
but seeing reporters in the garden,
she ducks next door. She and Aline plot
how tomorrow in the dusty air under the trapeze
they will not open their arms for Isabelle.
No one will fly through the air unscathed.

Gold

A second Nobel medal is awarded to Marie Curie
for what she calls chemistry of the imponderable.
A letter follows the good news.
Madame Curie, truly we are grateful and amazed
that you found radium and polonium, new elements,
but you must understand that we cannot give a prize if
the scandal we heard is true:
you lunch with a married man.

The lines Mé likes to keep
are breaking
work   science   love.
She puts her hands over her ears
as Irène checks tickets and timetables.
No rose is pinned to Mé's waist
as they take the train to Sweden.
This time Marie Curie stands and speaks
of the hidden ways that power
makes itself known. An atom can change after all.

Returning to Paris, Irène leans against her mother,
careful of the arm she said was sore.
She turns over the gold medal
to a picture of a muse wearing a falling robe.

Mé tucks the medal back in her bag.
Work is the prize.

Of course, Irène says.

Someone with two Nobel Prizes
can afford to be humble.
Irène can't help thinking, *Someday I want my own.*

False Names

Mé conducts experiments,
reviews plans for a laboratory
to honor Pierre. Irène reminds her to eat breakfast,
sets out crusty bread and thick plum jam.
As her daughters
grow taller, Mé loses twenty pounds.
Her blond hair turns gray.
She falls and is carried to a hospital on a stretcher,
admitted under a false name. Strangers lean together,
turn their necks to whisper, *The sinner expects a baby*
though Mé is ill from a simple infection.
The Sisters of the Family of Saint Marie
offer water treatments, a darkened bedroom.
Mé refuses prayer but endures
skin peeling from her cracked fingernails, a cough,
the split between widow, lover, scientist, mother.

For almost a year, Irène and Eve live with Aunt Bronya,
who takes them to the shore. They swim past fishermen
spreading nets. Along the road, as horses pull wagons,
Irène tightens her hold on Eve's arm.
Watch where you step.

I know! I'm eight years old.

Yes, too old now for dolls, Irène tells her, and teaches
her to play tennis. She writes: *Mé, come home.*

Her mother finds new doctors, giving them her sister's
or dead mother's name—
Dr. Bronya Dluski, Madame Sklodowska—
so reporters can't find her.

Irène asks, *How can you take their names?*

They're just borrowed names.
I need privacy.

Fine, but don't forget who you are.
Don't give up your name. It's my name, too.

MAPS

The walls of the Radium Institute are freshly painted
when the German army invades France. Scientists
become soldiers. Mé lines a suitcase with lead
and packs all the country's radium—
about half a teaspoon—
to smuggle to a safe in Bordeaux.
Bombs explode over Paris
so Mé sends Irène, Eve, and the Polish cook and tutor
to the seashore. Eve climbs rocks she calls castles.
She still prefers the visible world:
the waves and shells,
not the forces that shape them.
Fine for her to play by water,
but Irène is sixteen—eager to study, work,
do more for France than knit socks for soldiers.
She hangs a map on the dining room wall,
sticks pins in the names of towns where battles rage,
marking regions that have been invaded;
will Poland ever again be free?
She reads novels that make her melancholy
and daydreams:
Will a boy ever stand close by my side, perhaps gazing
at an unordinary flame, its fierce heat constant?

Mé mails letters and mathematics problems,
geometric proofs.
Irène's answers to equations
involving the speed of light,
angles of glass, and refraction are impeccable.
Her letters get shorter each week:
Why can't I work with you in Paris?

I need you to look after Eve.

Irène seethes. *Why should I be hidden,*
like radium encased in lead?
Waves curl, crash. Pebbles cling,
then clatter back to the froth.

SECOND SUMMER OF THE WAR

With farmers gone to battlefields,
Irène helps harvest wheat.
She cuts grain and binds stalks into sheaves.
This blue air is too empty
while the sky over Paris explodes
with the ends of experiments.

Irène opens the newspaper, wonders, *How will historians
tell facts from lies, find truth in all the conflicting stories?*
How dare anyone invade France! How can she listen
to her sister mangle English tenses, dither through
Polish conjugations? What can she teach a girl
with no taste for abstractions? It lacks salt.
Does a hunger for pianos and pretty shoes prevent
Eve from knowing what can't be held within hands?
How can a girl survive in a world made of equations
she won't understand?

Irène reads that the wounded
die slowly from infections
begun by bullets doctors can't swiftly find. Mé writes
about how X-rays penetrate skin, faster than knives.
She describes how she looped her cracked leather bag
over her elbow and called on wealthy women to ask for

motorcars or money to buy them.
Red crosses are painted
on the doors of cars used to carry X-ray machines to
battlefields. Soon Mé has more cars than drivers.
And with no time to wait for someone else to fix parts,
she learns to change a flat tire and clean carburetors.
She trains nurses.

Irène writes, *Mé, please teach me to drive.*
I can take X-rays.
Her mother writes: *No.*

Irène is tired of picking blackberries. One night
jam stains the pot purple with foam when an old man,
red-faced, stinking of wine,
stumbles into the kitchen.
He's heard Josia, the Polish cook,
speak a language he doesn't know
and calls her a German spy.

Get out! All of Irène's anger rises.

The next morning, she strides
into the mayor's office.
Make sure this doesn't happen again.
That drunk should know our cook came from a country
that has been invaded, too.

Back at home, she tells Josia, *If someone breaks in,*
grab a broom, a pot, even a kitchen knife if
you need it. Irène is finished here. She has other places
to defend and the voice to do it.
She writes to her mother, *I am the age you were*
when you left home.
I'm coming to Paris to work with you.

SEEING INSIDE SOLDIERS

Driving twenty miles an hour,
Irène carries X-ray machines
past periwinkles and narcissus growing
at the edges of forests.
She is a scientist disguised as a nurse in a white robe,
her wiry curls covered like a nun,
a red cross sewn on her sleeve
as if only mercy, and not physics, were her work.

Near a battlefield in Belgium, Irène drapes
army blankets over windows to darken the clinic room.
She pulls on cotton gloves to protect her hands
and steps behind a wooden screen.
X-ray machines let her see past skin and muscles
to the beautiful bones of soldiers her age, carried
in on stretchers, sometimes missing arms or legs.
Some crawled out of lumbering metal tanks,
fired guns that spit ammunition faster
than fingers on triggers.

Irène touches the ripped flesh,
keeps her eye on the machine's revelations
of shell splinters, bullets, bomb fragments,
or simply the bones of a hand she will not hold.

Glancing at X-ray photographs,
she makes swift geometric calculations,
searching for sources of ruin or pain,
then tells a surgeon where to place his knife.

The doctor ignores her, moves his hand the other way
too fast, cruelly cuts. Only after he finds nothing
does he probe where she pointed
to four bits of shrapnel
among shattered bones.

On the evening of her eighteenth birthday,
Irène can't help wondering
if she will ever stand by someone
the way her mother and father stood in the shed
gazing at blue light. *Don't think about dancing.*
She knows biology: A heart can't really split.
Guns and cannons make her music as she eats alone.

EXAMS

In the Radium Institute library,
Irène puts articles in order
then helps her mother in the laboratory.
As they stand side by side,
the keys in their pockets clatter. Like Mé,
Irène favors loose black dresses that skim her ankles
where cotton stockings wrinkle.
To save time, they cut their own hair.

One day Irène sets down a beaker as she hears
cheers, cannon fire, people singing "La Marseillaise."
After fifteen hundred days of war, France is free.

About a million X-ray procedures
helped save thousands of lives.
Irène gets a military medal. Of course work
is the prize. She studies at the Sorbonne.
Taking her exams, she rubs the pencil
the way her mother rubs the sores on her hands
and fills in answer after answer
about mathematics, physics, and chemistry,
positive they are correct.

ELEMENTS

Irène and Mé avoid touching chemicals.
They wash their hands often.
Everything in the laboratory is labeled.
There are no spills.
But the pale skin on Mé's hands cracks, burns, peels
from what no one can see. Never mind:
Radium burns skin, but new skin grows.
Radium ravages cells,
so healthier cells may take their place.
Could this element cure terrible diseases?
Will the list of known elements keep expanding?
They have many questions
but little radium to use for answers.

Mé would trade her gold prizes for more.
Instead, her solitude is required,
her presence at grand tables under chandeliers.
She travels, giving speeches requesting funds
to buy the element she discovered
but can't afford. Irène believes her mother
would rather be back at the glass-roofed shed
stirring pitchblende, month after month, year after year.

Irène and Eve stay in the new apartment,
spare but for a grand piano
with scrolled legs. There are no carpets to be cleaned,
no curtains to cover a view
of the Seine, the Île-de-la-Cité.
In the evening, Irène watches seagulls
and tugboats on the river.
Eve practices complicated pieces on the piano.
Then writes notes of gratitude or condolence
for the mother and sister who cannot bear to say hello.

Mé returns, climbs three flights of stairs.
Her old brown bag is swollen with papers,
fading flowers,
gifts from admirers, tucked at her elbow.
A glaze, like ice, makes her eyes seem distant.
Irène unpacks her mother's honorary degrees,
medals, menus with calculations scribbled on the back,
gifts swathed in tissue paper,
bits of the humble amazing world:
petrified wood, rough woven wool, polished rocks.

CROSSING THE ATLANTIC

At a New York pier, a brass band celebrates the arrival
of the famous scientist. Mé tries not to look as if
she's leaning as she walks to the hotel
between Irène and Eve.
Roses crowd their room and spill into the hall,
sent by a florist whose cancer was cured by radium.

In packed halls, Mé lectures, coughs,
glances at notes she can barely
see with her cataract-clouded eyes. She twists
the facts of her life into a fairy tale:
The poor girl from Poland marries a prince of science.
After great struggle, they find
an element that saves lives.

Mé shakes hundreds of hands, grimly signs autographs.
Eve flirts with reporters, winks at toddlers,
coos at babies.
At elegant dinners she furtively moves the salt shaker
so Mé doesn't knock it over
reaching for the sugar bowl.
Mé presses her hands on her ears, complains of
an incessant humming. She visits doctors
who advise rest, perhaps stopping her work altogether.

While Mé receives treatments
for her twilight-colored eyes,
Irène takes her place at the podium. She lectures
about how invisible rays split and hidden energy
can grow enormous. Uncertainty nudges science
forward through risks, tricks, timing,
then, after long perseverance,
sometimes a stumble into luck.

In between talks, Irène and Eve play tennis.
They ride a Ferris wheel on Coney Island.
They take trains across the country
are sprayed by Niagara Falls
swim in Lake Michigan. Often, young men
gaze past Irène to her sister. Irène runs a hand
over her unruly brown hair, tells herself
Eve will find a beau before she does, making this a fact,
the end of an equation, which usually calms her.
I have my work. Someone must care for Mé.
Who has the time, anyway, for romance?

THE CANYON

Above the Grand Canyon, Irène calculates distances
while Eve buys a turquoise and silver pin.
They ride mules down narrow trails by ancient rock.

Reaching the river, Eve asks, *Have we ever been deeper?*
Irène paid attention to altitude in relation
to sea level, but Eve doesn't want numbers.
She crouches, dips her hands, says, *I remember*
Papa peeling an apple, letting skin spiral.
Once he pulled up my socks.

Irène's knees ache, but she stays still beside
her sister, who closes her eyes. *What acoustics!*
Eve spreads her arms as if she could hold
the gold and sepia strata.
Someday I will play the piano across Europe.

Brown-skinned men call the tourists back to the mules,
who bump one another on their leads. Irène turns
toward the animals, tells her sister,
We have so much work still to do.

PARIS

Irène and Mé now work side by side, though Irène
can't forget one of them
keeps two Nobel Prizes in her bureau.
Eve, now twenty-one, cuts her black hair in a bob,
hems her skirts higher, rouges her lips and cheeks,
draws kohl lines around her blue eyes.

Mé says, *Why must you torture your eyebrows?*
Those shoes! Women were not made to walk on stilts.

Irène keeps out of the conversation. Eve is Eve.
Why try to change her?
Eve throws on a wrap, steps out to the city
of *pâtisseries*, the Eiffel Tower,
window displays of lace and hats, paints and palettes,
impeccable gardens where children push sailboats
in a circular pool.
Swallows soar past cathedrals, where stained glass
splinters light. Eve will dine
with a young man for hours. She gives concerts
around the city and in the provinces.

Irène and Mé turn back to their own supper:
radishes, a wedge of cheese, and cherries,
with books propped open on the sugar bowl.

CONVERSATION

Irène warms her sore back on the radiator,
talks to colleagues about gamma rays,
alpha rays, electrons.
Radium tangles invisibly in her hair,
tucked behind her ears,
penetrates the creases in her knuckles.

Frédéric Joliot talks with such passion
that Irène never minds
his freshly ironed linen shirts,
the collars creased to points.
Dimples pierce his cheeks. Why shouldn't
he smile to show them off?
His dark fresh-trimmed hair
curls over his left eyebrow. Tall, lean, he bends
to hear more clearly as they speak
of fission, fusion, nuclei. *Is it possible*
to manufacture radium?
He says, *Your father was a genius.*
Irène smiles with her unpainted lips,
tucks her hands with their flaking skin
behind her back. Should she pin a rose to her waist? *No.*

LUNCH HOUR

Irène and Frédéric bicycle through parks
play tennis, each intent on winning.
They spread a blanket in a meadow for lunch.
He studies her face like an equation that puzzles
him, confident he'll reach answers. Soft cheese
puddles into black currants and plums.
Wasps claim a dab of gooseberry jam.
As they talk about experiments, his deep voice
thuds from his chest to hers. The broken end
of a baguette turns crusty.

As weeks of courting continue,
it becomes not so tiresome to say
bonjour or *au revoir* even to strangers.

Mé protests, *That man is too carefree, too vain.*

*You hired him yourself! Only the most brilliant
for the institute.*

He's too young for you.

Just three years. Papa was nine years older than you.

Irène becomes as certain of love as
she is of her calculations.

Their simple wedding is on their lunch hour.
Like her mother, she wears dark, practical clothes
and refuses a gold ring
she'd have to remove to work.
Something finer will shine from a beaker.

FINALLY

After Irène gives birth to Hélène,
Mé calls Frédéric by name instead of introducing
him as *the man who married Irène.* Mé celebrates again
when Irène gives birth to a boy
she names Pierre, after her father.
Each day Mé devotes half an hour
to her grandchildren.
She and Hélène watch snails squirm or clouds scuttle
through the illusion of blue sky:
refractions, reflections, radiance.

When it rains, they do puzzles at the kitchen table,
the faded oilcloth blurred from coffee stains.
Let no one say
Mé stumbles between science and love. She holds
the baby in a tender grip, though Irène spots weakness
in her thin shoulders. Everything can break.
History, science, gleaming glass beakers,
the shine of eyes growing dim.

SISTERS

Small Hélène sprawls on Irène's lap while she stirs
coffee, points out how milk swirls
the way electrons orbit a nucleus. When she
forgets to sip, Eve takes her cup, tucks
Pierre in his basket, rolls crepes she sprinkles
with soft white sugar for Hélène.

Eve won't be a concert pianist, claims,
I'm not good enough.
I'll play again, though maybe not on stages.
Instead, she reviews opera and theater,
escorts Mé to and from work.
When Mé crosses a street,
Eve clasps her elbow, pretending her grip
is all affection and not aid.

Triumph, 1934

Irène and Frédéric photograph
tracks of protons, neutrons,
and electrons. They count electric pulses
the charged aluminum silent until, after years
of experiments, the Geiger counter clicks
Ch-chu-chrrr
signaling radioactivity where no radium was present.
Frédéric cheers, leaps, tosses up papers of calculations.
Irène dashes downstairs to find her mother
who bends to hear small sounds
that show atomic nuclei are radioactive.
Matter is energy. Energy is matter.

Thirty-five years ago,
Marie and Pierre Curie discovered radioactivity.
Now Irène and Frédéric have made it artificially.
Standing side by side,
they barely move as Hélène nudges
between them. Irène picks her up.
A milky haze coats Mé's eyes,
which meet her daughter's. This gaze is her gold.
They boil water in flasks on a Bunsen burner,
pour tea to raise in a toast.

Never again must they stir pitchblende
or plead for gifts.
All the radioactive material scientists need can be made.
What was called impossible is not.
An atom can be split.

FLIGHT

Buttercup petals scoop yellow sun as Mé admits,
I'm tired. She agrees to let Eve
take her to a clinic in the mountains.
She will register as Madame Pierre:
No one must worry,
no one must guess the limits of science.
Irène gently touches Mé's frail shoulders,
her forehead, hot with fever,
then gives Eve a swift hug.
Hélène cries when her grandmother
says good-bye. To distract her, Irène crouches,
points out how ants hustle,
their jaws clamped on minuscule food and timber.
She tips a small stone. Spiders scuttle and scatter.
A snail, black antennae ornamenting its quiet head,
leaves a silvery trail as it crawls past poppies.
Little Pierre flaps his arms and screeches.
The snail stops, tucks in its head.

He's too noisy. Hélène glares at her little brother.

Irène hands her a green net to chase butterflies
that flit and fold their wings. Irène scoops
one with brown-gold spots and splotches from the net.

The rough velvet of its wings weighs almost nothing.
She opens her hands.

Don't let her go! Hélène protests.

It is as good to watch the butterfly disappear as to hold it,
Irène says, watching her daughter's eyes darken.
The muscles behind her knees pinch as she crouches
to fold her arms around this beautiful angry child.
Who can help wanting wings, soft as rose petals,
in her hands?

Handful of Dirt

White and blue birds call from trees
as the dirt above a pine casket is scraped away
to make room for another. Gone are the periwinkles,
yellow irises, the sweet-scented lilies
Mé scattered long ago.
Aunt Bronya drops a handful of Polish earth.

As Marie Curie wished, no men wearing crosses
or medals speak.
Irène can't keep her mind on a colleague's praise.
She rubs her fingers, faintly burned at the tips,
remembers,
We are very careful. Surely radium makes no one ill.
Her stockings wrinkle at her ankles,
the way her mother's had,
the way she believes stockings are meant to sag.
Eve's hat curves eloquently
over her blue grief-stricken eyes.
She folds her strong, soft hands
as a small dark stripe
zigzags across Irène's foot, then disappears.
The butterfly casts a long shadow.
Memory shifts like atoms.

Mé, come home, Irène wrote
in old letters she finds saved in a candy box
tied with thin ribbon.
Can the past press closer than the present?
Who is a daughter without a mother?

CEREMONY

Irène won't write a diary to the dead.
There is grief, but much left to discover and one day
even joy. Waving a letter, Frédéric shouts, *We did it!*

Irène's hands shake. What did she wish for?
There's still so much to do.
Pierre, is your hair combed? Did Hélène
have a chance to play in the yard today?
Irène races out to check the laboratory equipment
buy plain cloth for the kitchen table
to cover old stains, keep life as it was yesterday.

Irène will take her mother's flat black shoes, not
yet worn down at the heels. She refuses a new hat
for the trip to Sweden,
but Eve finds her a new black gown.

Don't go. Hélène stamps her small foot.

Irène soothes her. *Aunt Eve will stay with you.*

Eve says, *I'll make crepes with jam tonight.*

You mustn't spoil them. Immediately, Irène regrets
her tone. How many young men had Eve told
no or *wait?* How many concerts and chances

had she turned down to see that their mother safely
crossed the street and was never alone?

Eve raises her voice. *Of course I will spoil your children.*
I'll buy Hélène pink ribbons and lure her to the piano.
Little Pierre will eat nothing but pudding,
if that's what he chooses.

Irène takes her hand. *You gave too much.*

Music is meant to disappear, Eve says.
Our mother never will.
Now go speak. People will listen.
Even girls who haven't yet been born.

Irène slips a mathematics book in her bag for the train
and reception, where Frédéric can smile at strangers.
First he talks of science,
then it's her turn behind the podium.

Staring straight ahead, she understands, of course,
that work doesn't end.
Every answer raises new questions.
She will slip the gold medal behind her husband's socks
like the gray-eyed woman with stained hands
who marveled at the power of what can't be seen.
Irène will never forget how they stood side
by side, staring at bowls of blue light.

LEGACIES

AFTER FRANCE was invaded by Germany again and World War II began, Irène Joliot-Curie sent her children to the village by the sea where she and her sister had spent the beginning of World War I. She kept working in Paris and mailed letters with mathematics problems to Hélène.

Both Irène and Frédéric helped save people from Nazi persecution. When their children's lives seemed too much at risk, Irène made plans to escape the country with them. Hélène, who was about the age Irène had been at the start of World War I, begged to take her exams first. Right after she completed her tests, Irène filled a knapsack with water, bread, a change of clothes, and a mathematics book. While Frédéric continued underground work for the French Resistance, Irène and their two children hiked through the Alps, arriving safely in Switzerland on June 6, 1944. They didn't yet know that American troops were landing on the beaches in Normandy that same day, D-day, helping to bring the long war to an end.

Eve Curie worked as a journalist through the war years, risking her life to bring back news from battlefronts around Europe. She wrote an acclaimed biography of her mother, and traveled more than 40,000 miles in Africa, the Middle East, the Soviet Union, China, India, and elsewhere as a reporter. She visited more than a hundred developing countries, working for UNICEF to improve children's health and educational opportunities. In 1954, she married Henry Labouisse, whose work as UNICEF director was honored with a Nobel Prize for Peace.

After World War II, Irène and Hélène, who was beginning her own distinguished career as a physicist, ran experiments together. Both Irène and Frédéric Joliot-Curie died of diseases brought on by their long exposure to radium. Their two children carried on their work.

TIME LINE

1867   Laura Ingalls is born in a log cabin in Wisconsin on
February 7.
Marie (then called Manya) Sklodowska is born on
November 7 in Warsaw, Poland.
Sarah Breedlove is born in a single-room cabin
near a Louisiana cotton plantation on
December 23.

1870   Laura and her family take one of many westward
journeys in a covered wagon, settling for a while
in Kansas.

1874   Sarah's parents die of yellow fever. With no
opportunity to attend school, young Sarah picks
cotton for a living, as her parents, former slaves,
had.

1878   Marie's mother, who'd been a teacher before
        contracting tuberculosis, dies. Marie tries to ease
        her grief with books and mathematics.

1879   The pioneering Ingalls family settles near Silver Lake
        in the Dakota Territory.

1882   Sarah marries Moses McWilliams, later saying,
        "I married at the age of fourteen in order to get
        a home of my own."
        Laura begins work in one-room schoolhouses.

1885   Laura marries Almanzo Wilder, after he courts her by
        offering rides home in horse-drawn buggies or
        sleighs.
        Sarah gives birth to A'Lelia (then called Lelia)
        on June 6 in Vicksburg, Mississippi.

1886   Laura gives birth to Rose on December 5 in what is
        now De Smet, South Dakota.

1891   Marie moves to Paris, France, to study science
        at the Sorbonne.

1894   The Wilders purchase a forty-acre farm with a creek,
        apple trees, and a log house in Mansfield, Missouri.

1895   Marie marries Pierre Curie, who shares her passion
        for science.

1897   Marie gives birth to Irène on September 12 in Paris,
        France.

1898   Marie and Pierre Curie discover and name the
        elements polonium and radium.

1903	Marie Curie, Pierre Curie, and Henri Becquerel win the Nobel Prize in Physics for their work on radioactivity.
1904	Marie gives birth to Eve on December 6. Rose leaves home to work as a telegraph operator in Kansas City, Missouri.
1905	Sarah uses her savings of one dollar and fifty cents to create the Wonderful Hair Grower.
1906	Sarah marries C. J. Walker and begins calling herself Madam C. J. Walker. After her husband dies in an accident, Marie expresses her pain in a journal she keeps for about a year.
1909	Rose marries Gillette Lane in San Francisco, California. A'Lelia marries John Robinson in a Pittsburgh courthouse, forming a union that lasts about a year.
1911	Irène accompanies her mother to Stockholm, Sweden, where Marie is awarded the Nobel Prize in Chemistry, becoming the first person to receive two Nobel Prizes.
1912	Madam C. J. Walker divorces her husband, but keeps the name she took when they married. A'Lelia adopts thirteen-year-old (Fairy) Mae Bryant.
1914–15	Seventeen-year-old Irène oversees a radiological center at a time when tens of thousands of French soldiers are dying on World War I battlefronts. Irène returns to Paris to train people to use X-ray

machines, work at the recently completed Radium Institute, and study at the Sorbonne.

1915   Madam C. J. Walker travels across the country with granddaughter, Mae Bryant, giving lectures about hair products and African-American successes since the Civil War. They attend a world's fair, the Panama-Pacific International Exposition, in San Francisco.
Rose Wilder Lane works as a reporter for the *San Francisco Bulletin*. When her mother visits, seeing California for the first time, they tour the Panama-Pacific International Exposition.

1917   After the United States enters World War I, Madam C. J. Walker and A'Lelia join the Circle for Negro War Relief and other causes to help African-American soldiers.

1918   Irène receives a bachelor of science degree from the Sorbonne.
Rose and Gillette Lane divorce. She keeps his last name and begins a long period of devoting herself more to friendships than family.

1919   Madam C. J. Walker dies of kidney failure on May 25. She bequeaths tens of thousands of dollars to charities, political organizations, and schools.

1920   Rose starts work as a foreign correspondent for the American Red Cross and Near East Relief, writing from the deserts of Egypt, the mountains of Albania, Greek islands, and cities including London, Paris, Rome, Vienna, and Athens.

1921   Marie, Irène, and Eve sail to the United States, where
        Marie and Irène lecture to raise money to buy
        radium.

1925   Irène defends her doctoral dissertation in front of a
        thousand people packed into a lecture hall at the
        Sorbonne and is awarded a PhD.

1926   Irène marries Frédéric Joliot in a civil ceremony on
        October 4.

1927   Irène Joliot-Curie gives birth to Hélène Joliot-Curie.

1931   A'Lelia Walker dies of a cerebral hemorrhage
        at age forty-six.

1932   Laura Ingalls Wilder is sixty-five when the first book
        bearing her name, *Little House in the Big Woods*, is
        published.
        Irène gives birth to a boy named Pierre, after her
        father.

1934   Irène and Frédéric discover how to make artificial
        radioactivity.
        Marie Curie dies in the French Alps of leukemia
        brought on by exposure to radium.

1935   Irène and Frédéric Joliot-Curie are awarded the
        Nobel Prize in chemistry for their discovery of
        artificial radioactivity.

1943   Laura's eighth book, *These Happy Golden Years*, is
        published. She decides to retire, though she
        continues to correspond with her many fans.

1949   Almanzo Wilder dies of a heart attack at home in
         Missouri.

1956   Irène Joliot-Curie dies of leukemia, brought on by
         work with radioactive elements.

1957   With her daughter by her side, Laura Ingalls Wilder
         dies on February 10, three days after her ninetieth
         birthday.

1958   Frédéric Joliot-Curie dies of liver failure, brought on
         by exposure to radioactive elements.

1968   Rose Wilder Lane dies at age eighty-two and is
         buried in Mansfield, next to her parents.

2007   Eve Curie Labouisse, writer, philanthropist, and
         acclaimed biographer of her mother, dies in New
         York City.

SELECTED BIBLIOGRAPHY

As with any biographical writing, much is left out of these lives shown in verse. I focused on turning points in the mother-daughter relationships and on the women's work. I hope readers curious to learn more will use this bibliography for suggestions of further reading. (Books noted with * were written specifically for young readers.)

ROSE WILDER LANE *and* LAURA INGALLS WILDER

Hill, Pamela Smith. *Laura Ingalls Wilder: A Writer's Life.* Pierre, SD: South Dakota State Historical Society Press, 2007.
Holtz, William. *The Ghost in the Little House: A Life of Rose Wilder Lane.* Columbia, MO: University of Missouri Press, 1993.
Miller, John E. *Becoming Laura Ingalls Wilder: The Woman behind the Legend.* Columbia, MO: University of Missouri Press, 1998.
Zochert, Donald. *Laura: The Life of Laura Ingalls Wilder, Author of* The Little House on the Prairie. New York: Avon Books, 1976.

A'LELIA WALKER *and* MADAM C. J. WALKER

*Bundles, A'Lelia Perry. *Madam C. J. Walker: Entrepreneur.* New York: Chelsea House, 1991.

Bundles, A'Lelia. *On Her Own Ground: The Life and Times of Madam C. J. Walker.* New York: Scribner, 2001.

Marks, Carole, and Diana Edkins. *The Power of Pride: Stylemakers and Rulebreakers of the Harlem Renaissance.* New York: Crown Publishers, 1999.

IRÈNE JOLIOT-CURIE *and* MARIE CURIE

Brian, Denis. *The Curies: A Biography of the Most Controversial Family in Science.* Hoboken, NJ: John Wiley and Sons, 2005.

Curie, Eve. *Madame Curie: A Biography.* Trans. by Vincent Sheean. Garden City, NY: Doubleday, Doran and Company, 1937.

Curie, Marie. *Pierre Curie.* Trans. by Charlotte and Vernon Kellogg. New York: Macmillan, 1923.

Goldsmith, Barbara. *Obsessive Genius: The Inner World of Marie Curie.* New York: W. W. Norton, 2005.

*Krull, Kathleen. *Marie Curie.* New York: Viking, 2007.

*McClafferty, Carla Killough. *Something Out of Nothing: Marie Curie and Radium.* New York: Farrar, Straus and Giroux, 2006.

McGrayne, Sharon Bertsch. *Nobel Prize Women in Science: Their Lives, Struggles, and Momentous Discoveries.* New York: Birch Lane Press, 1993.

Pflaum, Rosalynd. *Grand Obsession: Marie Curie and Her World.* New York: Doubleday, 1989.

*Pflaum, Rosalynd. *Marie Curie and Her Daughter Irène.* Minneapolis, MN: Lerner Publications Company, 1993.

Quinn, Susan. *Marie Curie: A Life.* New York: Simon and Schuster, 1995.

PHOTO CREDITS

Made in United States
North Haven, CT
02 April 2022